LESSONS FROM THE BACK OF THE LINE

How Teachers Change the Trajectory of Lower Income Students

BY JOSHUA C. DUNCAN

Inspired Forever Book Publishing

Dallas, Texas

Lessons from the Back of the Line
How Teachers Change the Trajectory of Lower Income Students

Inspired Forever Book Publishing
Dallas, Texas
(888) 403-2727
https://inspiredforeverbooks.com

Printed in the United States of America

Library of Congress Control Number: 2020901984

ISBN-13: 978-1-948903-06-6

Disclaimer: this book reflects the author's recollections of experiences over time. Some names and characteristics have been changed to protect privacy, some events have been compressed, and some dialogue has been recreated.

DEDICATION

Our public school system isn't perfect, but that isn't a reflection of the great staff, teachers, and administrators who give it their all day in and day out. I want to personally thank every great teacher across the world for sacrificing so much to give our youth a better future. Often, we spend more time with our students than their parents do. We have the power to inspire the next presidents, astronauts, and Nobel prize winners. We also know that the opportunity to positively impact our great nation starts when the bell rings and that first child walks through the door. Fellow educators, keep on keepin' on!

I also want to dedicate this book to the great students and future leaders I had the opportunity to teach as well as to my aunts, cousins, sister-in-law, and family friends who inspired me to choose such a rewarding path. I'd like most of all to thank God for the opportunity, the inspiration to write with purpose, and the platform to inspire positive reform in the educational system.

TABLE OF CONTENTS

INTRODUCTION:

MAN ON A MISSION

Once upon a time, I was a lower income student living with extended family members because my parents and two of my three older brothers were in and out of jail. With a lot of help, I went to college and became an elementary school teacher. My success was anything but guaranteed, and I'm not alone.

According to the National Center for Educational Statistics, between 2015 and 2016, there were about 89,000 public and private elementary schools in the United States. As of the fall of 2018, 35.6 million elementary age students were enrolled in public school alone. Nearly 15 million of those students—21% of all children in the U.S.—live in families with incomes below the federal poverty threshold.

I wrote *Lessons from the Back of the Line: How Teachers Change the Trajectory of Lower Income Students* for the nearly 3.2 million elementary, middle school, and secondary public and private teachers, plus the staff and administration, who work across our great nation. This inspirational memoir highlights tales of students and teacher overcoming obstacles and inspiring one another. Of necessity, these stories dive deep into poverty, bullying, suicide, crime, abuse, and more because what happens outside the classroom impacts what happens inside.

I taught third, fourth, and fifth grades at a lower income elementary school in Dallas, Texas, for four and a half years, from 2012 to 2016. In 2012, to begin combatting the extraordinary need I saw, I founded a nonprofit organization called MJD Community Solutions, eventually renamed Camp AHA, which stands for Active-Healthy-Academic. Each summer, students between the ages of seven and 12 gathered at Camp AHA to learn about the importance of staying active, healthy, and focus on academics. Campers played basketball, soccer, and friendly competitive games. They ate foods that are nutritious while learning to avoid foods that are detrimental to their health. They learned grammar through reflection, math through budgeting, business through working with community leaders, and science through experiments with food. Camp was full of positive music and creative arts.

Today, Camp AHA has transformed into Ascension Leadership Group, a mentorship program for underprivileged youth, connecting leaders of the classroom with leaders in their community. Mentors receive encouraged curriculum similar to that of the original summer Camp AHA and sponsorship funds are raised to send these amazing students to reputable summer camps that surround them with other great kids and expose them to the amazing opportunities they have in life.

I left teaching in 2016 to build a marketing firm founded in the Dallas/Fort Worth area focused on brand modernization. By combining my twin passions of education and marketing, the goal is to build my reputation and resources throughout the business world, reach a larger number of students, and ultimately make a bigger impact than I could by remaining in a single classroom. In addition to speaking engagements with disadvantaged college students and marketing presentations in the city's tallest buildings, I hope to begin speaking at teacher workshops, presenting tools that can help teachers overcome the challenges their impoverished students face while teaching them the skills it takes to be successful.

The battle going on inside the minds of lower income students can only be addressed by teachers and administration who have extremely high expectations paired with techniques to bring these students up to par. *Lessons from the Back of the Line* explores the effects of low income, lack of sleep, lack of health care, hunger, poor quality of life, tattered clothing, incarcerated family members, and more. It offers concrete, practical techniques for addressing these effects, giving an insider's view on how to lift up and empower lower income youth.

My goal in this book is to inspire educators, teachers, staff, and administration by bringing to light the realities and opportunities that come with teaching students in lower income classrooms. By offering my perspective on this vital work, sharing firsthand stories of struggle, and narrating lessons that resulted in student growth, I hope to help educators across the globe better connect with their students. When we understand what is going on in the minds of children who live in poverty, we can make a significant difference.

Our lower income students receive free clothes, backpacks, supplies, and food, yet many have iPhones and the newest pair of Jordans. In spite of these material possessions, their likelihood of escaping the vicious cycle of poverty is slim to none. While material possessions are great, they are temporary. Impoverished students require knowledge they can only acquire through great teaching and mentorship from teachers and others who can adapt to each child's unique learning style while addressing the ongoing challenges they face.

Lessons from the Back of the Line also uncovers the pressures teachers face in a society that asks questions like, "Why teach when you can earn a greater salary elsewhere?" and "How do great teachers find themselves in classrooms instead of corporate America?" I wrote this book to tell the story most teachers do not have the voice or time to tell.

On the one hand, teachers hear statements like "Teachers are so important. They change the world."

On the other hand, we hear ourselves say things like, "We should get paid more," "Our workload is too much," "We are underappreciated," and "We don't have enough help."

The truth is, most in the corporate world look down upon educators, and this is inexcusable. We need to highlight the vital role we play in the crucial process of helping lower income students develop the skills they need to defy the odds stacked against them. Teachers are on the front lines in the battle against poverty, crime, and the vicious cycle of struggle generations of lower income families face.

For teachers looking to expand differentiation skills and tailor their instruction to meet individual needs, this book is for you. The fact is, when your students do not care to pick up a pencil and try, how does teaching them a new method of 2 + 2 make a difference? *Lessons from the Back of the Line* explores why students don't try and gives tips to overcome this common problem.

Ready to jump into real stories of real students interspersed with my story and how it inspired me to enter the elementary school classroom and teach differentiated lessons? Let's meet a few students and dig into the struggles they faced to become great inside the classroom and out.

From educator to executive, my mission is to bring awareness to the opportunities underprivileged youth have to become successful through knowledge and mentorship and to inspire my fellow teachers to do all they can, every single day, to help these kids who so desperately need and deserve it.

CHAPTER 1:

YOU WANT TO BE AN ELEMENTARY SCHOOL TEACHER?

Education is the most powerful weapon
which you can use to change the world.

Nelson Mandela

In college, once I completed every class required to receive my education degree, I was ready to graduate, right?

Wrong. The final task before I became the first person in my immediate family to graduate from college was student teaching.

Technically, student teaching is a class, but this class was nothing like the others I'd taken. It included a semester at a campus chosen for me and was meant to slowly but surely teach me how to successfully manage my own classroom by implementing the skills and strategies I'd been taught at college into real-life situations with living and breathing children. About 20 of them, to be exact. No pressure, right?

I had envisioned myself instructing fourth, fifth, or even sixth graders. At this age, students can handle basic responsibilities and manage their own classwork. With a nod to all the men out there, this means these students do not require babying. A room full of babies ranks right next to death and public speaking when it comes to the top fears among men.

I was all set, or so I thought. Then, a couple of weeks before the beginning of the new school year, I received an email that read, "Mr. Duncan, your placement will be at Chandler Elementary. You will be student teaching first grade with Ms. Barbara Laura."

First grade? Was someone playing a trick on me? What was I going to do with a room full of five- and six-year-olds? I reluctantly accepted my placement, and two weeks quickly passed.

My "first day of school" was the thirty-second "first day of school" for my mentor teacher. Barbara Laura was a short lady, soft spoken, with a gleam of kindness in her eyes. Her calmness reminded me of a still quiet pond with the morning sunrise peeking around the corner.

On the other hand, I was afraid for my life as I stood in that classroom, anxiety spreading through every cell of my body.

I'm prepared for this. This is what I studied for. It will all fall in place, I told myself. Students would be entering the room in five minutes with backpacks, supplies, and a surplus of eagerness. Parents would introduce themselves, ask questions, and say goodbye to their young scholars.

I had no time to waste, so I introduced myself. "Hi, I'm Joshua Duncan, your student teacher. Please let me know what I can do to help you."

"The morning work is already on the desks," she told me. "As the students come into the room, make sure they find their name tags and get started on their assignments. Help only when completely necessary. I want to practice maturity and independence from the very first day."

We were working with six-year-olds, and I was thoroughly impressed. Each desk had been assigned to a specific student, and each child's take-home folder was already placed neatly inside his or her desk with important papers for parents to sign. Mrs. Laura's preparation and confidence were as contagious as a yawn and could not have come at a better time. The bell rang, students were on their way, and now that I thought about it, I actually felt ready. I mean, how difficult could it be to teach first graders?

The evening before, I'd spoken on the phone with Aunt Kim, a veteran teacher herself. I told her the big day was tomorrow and asked if she had any advice, and her words were golden.

"The person you'll be learning from won't be perfect. You'll probably have different opinions, ideas, and techniques, and this is okay."

Her words helped calm the butterflies in my stomach.

She continued, "But there will be several great ideas and routines you'll find to your liking. When you create your own classroom, you can implement them. There's an incredible amount to learn. Enjoy it, because it will be over before you know it!"

Although I appreciated Aunt Kim's encouragement, I tossed and turned all night. In spite of my desire to teach, every now and then I questioned myself. Was this really what I was supposed to be doing? I was a 6'6, 220-pound man whose best friends were pursuing careers in medicine, law, engineering, and business. They were going for the big bucks while I was choosing to be a teacher, and not just any teacher—I was choosing to teach elementary school. According to the National Education Association, in the year 2017, only one-fourth of the teachers in U.S. public schools, including high schools, were male. In elementary and middle schools, the numbers dropped even further, to just over 20%. Many students graduated from a public high school without ever having a single male teacher!

Why had I chosen this career path? Could I handle the pressure of doing something few men could? I recalled how, when I'd approached active teachers and expressed my interest in teaching, they'd often told me to do something else, something more socially acceptable for males. Suggestions ranged from "Why not pursue business?" to "I can see you being a great lawyer" to "You're not coaching? Elementary school, huh?"

Needless to say, these exchanges could have caused me to abandon teaching, but I deliberately tuned them out. Now, here I was, inside a first grade classroom, doing my student teaching.

The first couple of weeks came and went faster than the weekends. The work was exciting, demanding, and filled with challenges. One Friday night that semester, I wrote about my experiences up to that point and a topic that had begun to consume me: discipline.

I'm two weeks into my new lifestyle. A 6:30 a.m. wake-up time allows me to start each day without rushing. A sense of maturity surrounds me as I am single, working, and maintaining my daily routines, essentially taking the first steps to becoming an adult. I continue to practice taking the best from every moment and finding the positive in all situations. Working with students who are growing into future leading citizens of our free democracy inevitably affects who I am developing into. Daily interaction with nearly 20 different personalities, all of whom look up to me, demands a heavy amount of discipline.

A recent verse I stumbled upon is, "To learn, you must love discipline; it is stupid to hate correction." To me, discipline isn't a repercussion for misbehavior; it's the root of each and every person's ability to master who they are.

At 6:30 a.m., when the dying goose screams through the alarm speaker, I am up without a second thought of snoozing. Reaching from my bed, I put the iPod on shuffle, serenading the first 30 minutes of my morning with rhythm. Slacks, sleek loafers, and a dress shirt complete the wardrobe as I finish up my oatmeal. The drive to work consists of windows down and music up. It's not often you can drive to work in perfect 65- to 75-degree weather without the west Texas sun baking everything it touches. At 7:35, I walk up to my assigned school. This walk occasionally makes me think of my freshman year of college when I chose to become an educator over a businessman, confidently accepting the annual pay of around $45,000.00. I look at the black Lexus GX sitting gallantly across the street.

Discipline:

At 7:45 a.m., like rain trickling on a windshield, individuals begin filling the room. She is interested in learning but shy around others. He glares during class activities and is lost in space for minutes at a time. She is talkative and loves sharing family stories. He is smart yet an instigator. She is behind her peers but tries harder than anyone else. He is extremely shy but observant. She stands

11

confidently but never says a word. He is energetic and happy, smart and quick, yet won't do a second of work without being forced. She is the attention getter, consistently creating situations that demand eyes on her and get her in trouble. He is smart and funny and has a noticeable speech impediment but talks more than most. She is always interested in what's going on, often asking questions like, "How did you get that tall?" He is complementary, smart, and respectful. She is a clown, always making faces and trying to make others smile. He's the oldest and acts like it; he knows it all. She is the tallest, most mature, and quickest to give a helping hand. He is small, quiet, and nice. She has an extremely keen conscience. He is a character, funny and loud but not on purpose. She has a unique imagination and is an artist.

Simple descriptions based on two weeks of knowledge cannot begin to capture these individuals. Deciding how to interact with each of them and creating an optimal learning environment takes patience, understanding, and selflessness. I'm beginning to grasp the fact that these children come from 19 different backgrounds and have been raised in 19 different ways. At school, these different per-sonalities mix in one room, but this is minuscule compared to how they will interact with others as they age and mature.

Discipline is wisdom, and wisdom is sparked by learning. I've already learned a great deal by working with each one of these stu-dents. I want to build their self-confidence so that they believe they can become something great. I spend more time with these children than most of their parents spend with them. Shouldn't education be the last thing to be cut from our national budget?

Discipline.

The following Cherokee parable about two wolves helps explain why I stood my ground and became an educator:

An old Cherokee was teaching his grandson about life. "A fight is going on inside me," he said to the boy. "It is a terrible fight and it is between two wolves. One is evil—he is anger, envy, sorrow, regret, greed, arrogance, self-pity, guilt, resentment, inferiority, lies, false pride, superiority, and ego." He continued, "The other is good—he is joy, peace, love, hope, serenity, humility, kindness, benevolence, empathy, generosity, truth, compassion, and faith. The same fight is going on inside you—and inside every other person, too." The grandson thought about it for a minute and then asked his grandfather, "Which wolf will win?"

The old Cherokee simply replied, "The one you feed."

I had a choice. On the one hand, I could feed the evil wolf with negative comments like "Consider the low pay," "You need more money so you can buy a nice car and a big house," "I could never deal with kids screaming and crying all day," and "What beautiful woman wants to marry a teacher?"

Or I could feed the good wolf with comments from friends and family such as, "Wow, these children will be so blessed to have you!" and "You are going to be an amazing role model!" and "You have a lot to give these kids."

I also fed the good wolf with comments by great teachers who said, "You've chosen such a rewarding career path. The results and progress are more fulfilling than you can possibly imagine."

Which wolf won the battle?

The one I fed. I pushed out the negative and fed the positive.

CHAPTER 2:

WELCOME TO MR. JOSH DUNCAN'S JOURNEY TO GREATNESS

The most beautiful people we have known are those who have known defeat, known suffering, known struggle, known loss, and have found their way out of the depths. These persons have an appreciation, a sensitivity, and an understanding of life that fills them with compassion, gentleness, and a deep loving concern. Beautiful people do not just happen.

Elisabeth Kübler-Ross

Feet scuffled, preceded by deep voices mumbling.

Who could be knocking at the door?

Three knocks, and a single voice silenced everyone inside with "Shut up!"

Metal slid, turned, and clicked.

"I'm just here for my kid and that's all," the man knocking at the door explained.

"What kid?"

"I know my kid is here; all I want is the kid," the determined father replied.

The man inside the house held a gun near his waist. Pulling the door open, he pointed to the back room.

Adrenaline flowed through the father's veins as instinct took over, guiding him straight to his son with zero disregard for the danger he was in.

Found in a tattered crib, Joshua was alive but not well.

Further evaluation revealed what happens to a child living in a drug house.

Ringworms infected the child's arms, stomach, back, and legs. Lice contaminated his long brown hair. Sores spread across his body.

That was then. This is now.

Statistics suggest that children who face adversity the moment they leave the womb won't be successful in a world where every odd is stacked against them, but sometimes these children are successful.

What makes one child choose a different path than his peers and family members? Is it a mentor who encourages a morally sound path? Is it a teacher who influences this child to tap into greatness? Is it something beyond the control of any one man or woman?

The question of how young people come to choose the road less traveled when the easy path, the path that's already paved, is filled with negativity, substance abuse, and a pervasive sense of being victimized is the Golden Ticket into Willie Wonka's Chocolate Factory. It even offers access to the sword in King Author's court. Figuring out how to help these kids is a tough cookie, to say the least, but dive with me into this Pandora's box.

In sharing my journey, I hope to shed light on how negative experiences led to positive outcomes for my students and me. In the end, they allowed me to teach students in my lower income classroom to embrace who they are and rise above adversity.

Against All Odds

I spent the majority of my elementary years living with my grandparents. Sometimes I lived with my dad, usually whenever he remarried or had a new girlfriend, but then something would happen and I'd move back to Grandma and Grandpa's. For a memorable period when my brothers and I were living with my dad, my Great uncle, my Grandpa's brother, moved in with us.

My grandfather had dropped out of school at age 15 and worked as a bus driver. His father was an abusive alcoholic who lacked the ability to properly care for his family. My grandpa could not read or write very well, but he did read us his Bible each evening, each word separated by entire seconds as he looked through the thick reading glasses leaning off his nose.

My patience as a restless boy ran short; it was impossible for me to sit still and listen.

Not surprisingly, my grandpa struggled to help me with my homework. Even when he understood it, he struggled to teach it, and instead ended up writing down the answers for me.

Grandma worked all day and into the evenings. When she came home, she made dinner, cleaned, and did the laundry for three grandkids. (My oldest brother came and went but seldom lived with us.) Rarely did she have a break to assist me with schoolwork. Home simply didn't provide academic support, but it was filled with love.

Learning my ABC's was my earliest frustration. Thinking I was clever, I asked myself, "Why do I need to listen when I already know the answer?" The way I saw it, the alphabet phonemic pattern was quite simple. Every letter made the noise it started with. "C" made a "seee" noise and "F" made an "eee" noise and "G" made a "jaa" noise and so on.

The confusion didn't stop there. The ABC song was a nightmare. My first grade teacher called my grandparents and father one evening to tell them I didn't know the alphabet. Their response was, "Are you crazy? Of course he knows the alphabet!"

That evening, Grandma said, "Now, Joshua, sing me the alphabet song and say each letter of the alphabet clearly."

I began with the tune of "Twinkle Twinkle Little Star." Every letter was perfection until I reached "K," but a long and unique letter of the alphabet approached. I swore that letter was "Eleminopee." I said it confidently and finished off with "Q-R-S-T-U-V-W-X-Y- and Z."

"Can you say it again and slow down after K?" Grandma asked.

I repeated the alphabet, slowing down as requested. "...H...I...J...K...Eleminopee... Q...R..."

"Wait, wait, wait." Grandma repeated herself for some odd reason. At the moment, I wasn't sure why. I knew the entire alphabet, especially the funny sounding letter "Eleminopee."

My brother stepped in, slowly repeating, "Elllll Emmmmm Ennnnn Ooooo Peeeee." Were these people crazy? They were repeating back to me a letter I already knew, and they were repeating it so slowly!

How many times have you seen this in your classroom? For some reason we think slowly repeating the same thing over and over will solve the misunderstanding. This is similar to pushing a button on the TV remote when the battery is low. Pushing the button harder does not make a difference in the power level of the battery.

Eventually, the alphabet made sense, but by the time I understood that my single letter "Eleminopee" was actually made up of five separate letters, I was so frustrated at how slowly everyone was talking that I denied my confusion and said I was just playing with them.

Nonetheless, once I mastered the alphabet, I did well in school. Perhaps my early success could be attributed to my attraction to challenges. I used to watch my grandma solve word searches and crossword puzzles. I would look at her puzzles and decide they were impossible to understand. At that point, I deemed Grandma a genius.

Word searches weren't as tough. I spent hours at a time on them until my eyes begin to ache and I saw double. I enjoyed the challenge and the feeling of accomplishment that came with finding hidden words.

Grandma also enjoyed jigsaw puzzles, especially during holiday seasons. I would sit with her at the dining room table for hours, shuffling through piece after piece, until I began to visualize and recognize shapes.

These simple challenges helped turn me into a problem solver. Later, when I received a challenge in class such as reading an article and then answering questions about it, it was just like the word searches and puzzles I had practiced so attentively. When I received a math word problem, I was confident enough to break it down into something I could understand and solve.

It's amazing how something as simple as having the patience to put together a puzzle could significantly increase my ability to solve a word problem, but it did. I had plenty of challenges, but I had helpful influences, too.

Turns out, they were enough to save me.

CHAPTER 3:

INCARCERATION, A WAY OF LIFE

Do not go where the path may lead,
go instead where there is no path and leave a trail.

Ralph Waldo Emerson

Today, I walk into every professional environment with my shirt tucked in and a smile on my face, making sure to look everyone in the eye. I do my best to remember each person's name and speak appropriately as I display the manners I've had the opportunity to learn.

Years at a private preparatory school prepared me for college. In college, I was a full-time student and part-time worker. Since I became an adult, everywhere I've lived has been extremely nice, and I'm confident I've not only had durable vehicles but also good-looking ones. I hold doors open for women, children, and even men. Although not everything in my life is perfect, just as the world isn't perfect, I walk around as if it is. I am an optimist.

Growing up, Batman was my favorite person other than my dad. I had Batman shirts, Batman toys, Batman movies, and even a Batman piggy bank in my collection. Every time I found coins and bills or was given money as a gift, I'd put it in my Batman piggy bank.

I don't remember how I heard the news that my father had been arrested. It could have been a call from him, information from my brothers, or maybe my grandparents or aunt told me. Either way, it was a devastating time in my life.

My dad has always been my true hero. When he was around, I followed him step by step. In pictures of me standing next to him, the look on my face is priceless. I was so proud to have him as my dad. He used to be a truck driver, and we would take trips around the country during the summers. There was no place in the world I would rather be than next to my father. Although he loved to play loud music at strange hours of the night and his tobacco smoke burned my eyes, I didn't care. I was just happy to be with him.

I wasn't sure how to feel when I heard he'd been arrested. The situation wasn't completely clear. If convicted and found guilty, he would be charged with his third felony. "Three strikes and you're out" meant he could be facing 20 years to life in federal prison.

Panic immediately set in. I was just a little kid. What if I never got to touch my father again? What if he spent the rest of his life behind bars and I could only see him through that clear scratched glass with a phone connected at each end?

My plan was to take all the money I'd saved up to that point and use it to bail him out. I was never much of a spender, so what I put into my piggy bank stayed put.

I counted the money. It was a total of $96.00 dollars. At my age, my perception of money was flawed. I thought $96.00 would be enough to get him out. My heart was crushed when I found out bail was thousands of dollars.

Sure enough, my dad sat in prison for about a year waiting for his trial to go to court. On top of that, we had to pay thousands of dollars for legal counsel.

Long story short, after a year, our family pulled enough money together to bail my dad out of jail and hire an attorney. Months later, we received the news that my father's case had been dismissed and he would be free of all charges.

Not surprisingly, working in a lower income school strongly correlates with the experience of seeing lower income parents arrested. What happens when one of your favorite students starts acting out because his father has been arrested and he has to live with Grandma? Do you tell him how sorry you are and talk about how hard his life must be? Or do you stare reality directly in the eye, break the situation down piece by piece, and teach him the tools he needs to function anyway?

One particular student was never in my class but stood out because of his strong personality during hallway passing periods. Basketball was his favorite sport, and I could relate. For a while, basketball was my life, and this kid was a reincarnation of me at a young age.

He saw me shooting baskets after school one day. After that, when my class passed his in the hallway, he would pretend to make a move and shoot a basketball over me. I would respond by slapping my hand forward in a defensive position. Then I would turn my hands into binoculars as I looked into the distance, trying to find where I'd blocked the ball. We would laugh and continue on.

In the middle of a lesson one day, a co-worker stopped by and asked if she could speak to me out in the hall. "You're pretty close to Rodrick aren't you?" she asked, a look of concern on her face.

I told her we connected well through sports and that I was a friend of his father's through pick-up basketball games after school.

She replied, "Perhaps you can talk to him. He's been acting up in class. I think it's because his father was recently arrested and Rodrick doesn't know what's going on."

I nodded and told her I'd talk to him when I had my off period. Although this was my only free time alone during the day, I always enjoyed working with students who needed a little extra attention.

I invited Rodrick to the library. We sat at a table and visited for a few minutes, and then I began to draw a family on a piece of paper. I drew the parents first. Under the mom I wrote the words "drugs," "prison," and "alcohol." Underneath the dad I listed "drugs," "prison," and "alcohol." I then drew four children.

On a separate sheet of paper, I drew a sketch of a different family along with their four children. Under the mom in this family, I wrote the word "lawyer" and under the dad I wrote "financial consultant."

"Take a look at each family's parents," I told Rodrick. "What do you think their children will be like?" I nodded in the direction of the incarcerated parents.

"I dunno, Mr. Duncan," he answered.

I hinted, "Do you think they will be just like their parents?"

Rodrick didn't say anything, so I nodded towards the second sketch and asked, "What do you think their children will end up doing with their lives?"

Rodrick was still quiet, so I said, "Let me tell you my story. My mom made bad decisions. She made a bad decision that put her in jail. My dad also made bad decisions that caused him to spend some time in jail. My parents had four children. Two of them have spent long periods of time in jail. Only one of my brothers and I are different. What do you think I decided to do? Did I follow the footsteps of my dad into prison?"

Rodrick shook his head, a smile beginning to form on his face.

"Did I follow the footsteps of my mom to jail?"

Rodrick shook his head again. His smile was bigger.

"Did I follow in the footsteps of two of my older brothers?"

Again, Rodrick shook his head no.

"So what did I do?"

"You became a teacher," Rodrick answered.

"And what else?"

"You sold tamales."

I nodded. "Anything else?" I continued to push him to dig deeper to recall my story.

"You have camps that kids can go to."

I nodded again. My students knew all about Camp AHA where I promoted active healthy academics.

"Is there more?" I kept pushing.

"You make websites! And you write those stories you read to us in class!" His voice was getting loud. I smiled and asked him to speak in a library voice.

"And you are kind of like a father..." Rodrick stopped and gave me a look that told me it was my turn to speak.

"When I was your age and didn't have help at home to do homework, do you think I said it was too hard? Did I earn zeroes by not turning it in?" I asked with the squinty eyes of an investigator.

He laughed and let out a chuckle. "No, sir."

"Did I say, 'You know what, my dad went to jail so I should just do the same thing?' No way!" I answered my own question. "But how often could I have given up on life when times got tough and gone to jail just like he did? My brothers did it, so why shouldn't I? Really, if they did it, why shouldn't I?"

The lesson was complete. Rodrick got it. His shoulders remained straight up, his attention dialed in.

I didn't tell him this story to boast about my success but to share my passionate pursuit of greatness. I wanted to show him that he too could take the "right" path and make it to the top. Once at the top, his own children would have a greater chance of remaining at the top, comfortably and happy, the ultimate goal in life.

Throughout the year, I continued to check on Rodrick. Unfortunately, his dad was not released before the last day of school. At a certain point, I quit asking him for updates, knowing he would share the news once it came. I also never asked for details. The purpose of working with him wasn't to find out specifics of his dad's case but to work on developing a positive mentality in a tough situation. My personal story provided the perspective of someone who had been in a similar situation but took a different path than my parents and siblings. I loved my parents and brothers, but I knew it was okay for me to be different from them. Rodrick needed to know this, too.

The most important lesson I aimed to teach Rodrick was self-awareness that he and he alone was in control of his actions, especially the decision to work hard in school and follow the rules rather than the footsteps of those who came before him. Most importantly, if by any chance he were to make the same mistake others made, I wanted him to understand that he alone would be to blame because he was the one who had made the decision and would suffer the consequences.

The response when other adults hear my story is usually astonishment. How could a boy growing up in such a harsh environment become a well-respected young man? Statistically, I'm an anomaly, and I feel blessed to be in the situation I'm in.

This is why I will always feel obligated to give back to kids who find themselves where I once was.

Many lower income students experience similar situations. You can help them even if you haven't personally experienced the incarceration of a loved one. Help your students think independently by encouraging their strengths. Ask about the awesome characteristics of their loved one who has gone to prison. Ask if they miss that person. Ask if they would want their child or sibling to feel the way they felt when they found out their loved one was behind bars. Then encourage them to make other choices.

Sympathy only goes so far. Action and empowerment changes lives.

CHAPTER 4:

ABANDONMENT'S PRETTY COMMON TOO

*What are you if the people who are supposed to love you
can leave you like you're nothing?*

Elizabeth Scott

"Do you ever regret not having your mom around? Do you feel like it's taken some sort of long-term emotional toll on you? Is it okay to talk about it?"

Friends and family seemed to be more curious than I was.

I could never say Mom came in and out of my life. The definition of "in and out" would mean I saw her on a somewhat regular basis, but this was never the case. Instead, she disappeared for years at a time. On occasion, she would call my brothers and me out of the blue, and at one point she sent a letter to me from prison that was sealed with bright red lipstick from her very own lips. That made me feel special.

It seemed as if she knew the Bible like the back of her hand, or at least she wanted me to think she did. Every time we spoke, she quoted verses and told me I was named after the biblical Joshua. Looking back, perhaps she wanted to make sure I chose a different path than she did.

My happiest moments with my mom came when I was about six. She begged my grandparents for an opportunity to visit and gave her word that she wouldn't take us away. With hesitation, my grandparents invited her to our house. I'm not sure why, but we always visited outside near the entrance.

I loved my mom. She was sweet. She was perfect to me. She would tell jokes and make me laugh. The sound of her voice soothed me, and when she left, I couldn't wait for her to come again. For a short time, she continued to come, and I began to feel I knew what a mom was. It was as if the love in my heart had waited until she was around to be released. Who cared if she'd been gone before? Now she was back, and I was happy!

My brother wasn't as excited or as quick to warm up. He was older than me by two years and understood more than I did. I remember him acknowledging our mother, giving his respect, and moving on with his own agenda, something that took him far away from her.

Soon, Christmas was around the corner, and what a miracle the end of the year was turning out to be. As we sat outside in lawn chairs, I remember hugging my mom and kissing her on the cheek. She asked me what was on my Christmas list, and I told her everything I wished for. Her smile and warmth were reassuring. She listened attentively and looked at me with such love. I didn't care if she bought me a gift; she was perfect!

We said our goodbyes, and she said she was looking forward to seeing me in a few days, just in time for Christmas.

The days came and went slower than an elderly slug with a back problem. Something about being young and anticipating moments of happiness stopped the world on its axis, miraculously hindering time from moving at its normal pace.

I woke up early Christmas Day. Although my grandparents were my true caretakers and loved me unconditionally, I looked forward to seeing my mom more than anyone else. Noon came without a sign or a phone call from Mom. We celebrated Christmas during the evening. Perhaps she'd come then? As more and more time went by, the heart I was wearing on my sleeve began to break. Finally, my grandpa walked out with an unwrapped box of games with wooden pieces. He told me my mom had dropped it off earlier but couldn't stay.

I opened the box, but I was crushed. I wanted to see Mom. I had learned to love her again, and now she was nowhere to be found.

In fact, she didn't come back for years. We got random phone calls from her, but it was never the same. I now understood why my brother acted the way he did. I didn't trust her anymore, but my feelings toward her never included anger. My heart was broken. I was disappointed and sad.

As I age and look back, I feel that my relationship with my mom is amazing. Through everything, from being abandoned at drug houses to sitting in the back of police cars to being raised by my grandparents, uncles, and stepmoms to attending nearly 10 different schools to moving in with my aunts to watching two of my three brothers follow the same path as our parents to moving to Austin and becoming independent at the age of 17, the lesson was Windex clear: life is not about the deck of cards you are dealt. It is about how you play your hand.

Happiness is all about perspective. So what if I didn't have a mom? I had so many more women in my life who loved me. My grandma was my mom. My aunts were my moms. My best friend's moms treated me like their own. Had my own mom been in my life, I would never have had the opportunity to be blessed by so many great women. The power of perception is unfathomable. Just as knowledge is not given freely, we must learn to be thankful for what we have.

I once asked my students, "Raise your hand if both your mom and dad still live together." Only a quarter of the class raised their hands. Public schools are full of unorthodox family situations. I then said, "Raise your hand if you live with your aunt and uncle." Then, "Raise your hand if you live with your grandparents."

We talked about how awesome it is to have these caretakers and how lucky we all were to have them. We talked about how some children don't have any family at all and how some children grow up in the foster care system, which has the potential to be nurturing but doesn't come with any guarantees.

I did my best to teach my students to look on the bright side, and I implore you to do the same. Kids can easily be blinded by losing their parents, but you can change their lives by showing them how to focus on the people who are in their lives, including their teachers, instead of the people who are not.

CHAPTER 5:

A STUDENT NAMED ANNA

Be so happy that when others look at you, they become happy too.

Yogi Bhajan

Long hair was the trend for girls. Often, ponytails were so thick that not even a needle could find its way through. Anna in particular had an assortment of colorful rubber bands lining every three inches of her hair until the tips delicately dispersed into thousands of strands.

Anna's big smile and look of excitement filled me with joy. She'd missed the first day of school, so on the second day, I rearranged the seating to give her a desk directly in the front row, next to the door. I told her I was excited she could join the class and that I was looking forward to the great year we were going to have. She responded with a shaky voice, shortness of breath, lengthy pauses between each word, and that same trademark smile from ear to ear.

"Me...too...Math...is...my...best...subject!"

My attention turned to the entire class and I continued my ritual beginning-of-the-year activities including an A–Z PowerPoint presentation telling the students about myself and how my unique path had led me to be their teacher. This was a fourth grade classroom filled with nine-year-olds, and each and every one of them was eager to see what Mr. Duncan, their first male teacher, was all about.

When the bell signaled it was time for students to rotate teachers, Anna was swarmed. The first girl grabbed her backpack, another walked behind her and stood waiting, and the third held on to her pencil bag and spiral notebooks. Anna smiled with her long ponytail hanging nearly halfway past her wheelchair as her friends rolled her out of the classroom.

Anna, my first physically handicapped student, helped teach me what it truly means to be great. She was easily one of my greatest inspirations, and I needed her. A classroom novice, I had plenty of challenges, but I was learning a lot from our school's veteran math teacher, who shared her personal tricks of the trade with me on a regular basis.

Our topic of conversation one day was why our country was falling behind academically on a global scale. We spoke of teaching techniques, curriculums, and the resources available to our students. These surely played a role, I mused, yet math could still be taught well enough without resources for students to succeed on a test. A great teacher and the desire to learn were most important.

At that moment, it came to me. The desire to learn was lower than it used to be. The expectation to learn was lower. Who was to blame for this plague sweeping urban public schools across

America? Was it the parents' fault? Was it the school's fault? Was it the government's?

Our youth, I decided, were becoming products of their environment. They were asking themselves, "What's the point of sitting down and deciphering the meaning of numbers when I can play a game on my new iPad?"

This mentality was one of the greatest battles I faced each year. Behavior issues, genuine misunderstandings, and various learning styles and paces couldn't compete with the difficulty brought on by a lack of effort. Every year I had at least five children who refused to do their math work. And then there was Anna.

The first few times we worked side by side, I wasn't sure how she was going to cope with the rigor of the classroom. Quick thinking and the ability to move from one activity to another in as little as five minutes were the norm. Would she be able to get enough practice with the whole group to success-fully complete independent work? Would I have to assign her a quicker and higher achieving student to be her study buddy so she could succeed?

Anna's list of possible excuses was limitless, starting with the fact that she was confined to a wheelchair and had difficulty speaking. She often became frustrated when her thoughts were quicker than her voice could articulate and would fight with all she had to get her words out.

Her fine motor skills were also compromised, and she strug-gled with the large accommodated writing paper, her shaking hand always beginning a downward spiral. The degree of focus and strength it took to hold a pencil was monumental. The extra squeezing and pushing broke the lead each time she attempted a new sentence. She even needed strong prescription glasses in order to see the writing on her paper. She had every excuse in the book to give up, but she never gave in.

Anna was a fighter. As soon as she came into the room each day and saw what I called the bell ringer question, she began the laborious process of putting pencil to paper. Letter by letter, number by number, she wrote. Sometimes I quizzed her verbally to alleviate the workload, but never once did I see a lack of effort.

Only a few weeks into the school year, she began refusing the assistance of her friends and independently guided her wheelchair through the hallways. When assignments were due, she would place hers neatly on her lap and roll to my desk, refusing to let another student take it for her. Once in a while, I would pretend she had run over my toe and would jump up and down howling "Aye yi yi!" She would laugh and giggle, letting me know such jokes were okay.

Each year, I challenged my students to create their own businesses. The year Anna was in my classroom, origami, rubber band bracelets, plastic lacing key chains, sewing, and foldable paper games were popular. Naturally, as a math and science teacher, I integrated math into these arts and crafts by asking the students to put a price tag on their products and to value them all the way to the hundredths place value. They also had the option of adding catchy slogans such as "Get it while it lasts."

After an hour of teamwork, creation, and pricing, I allowed five minutes for a trading period. Each student also had the option of keeping the items already in their possession. Students started with five dollars in play money and had the opportunity to "up sale." A few adjustments and redirections later, and the activity was a success. Students were excited to be in business and making deals with their friends.

"What type of deals did we make? Did anyone get any awesome new products?" I asked during our follow-up discussion.

Smiling, Anna raised her hand and volunteered to share her experience. Almost a full second elapsed between each word.

"I...bought...this...awesome... new... pink...phone!"

Her classmates began laughing as they looked at the bright pink paper handmade phone a fellow classmate had made.

"I...did...buy...one...get...one... half...off," she continued, holding up a sign.

"Very creative." I responded. "I didn't even think of that slogan. What a way to be a leader with that innovative idea!"

The Epiphany

ARD meetings, also known as Admission, Review, and Dismissal, are for parents and families of students who are eligible for special education support and services.

At the first meeting of the year, our special ed coordinator introduced everyone and explained, "This is a fairly new case, seeing that Anna developed the disability only this summer."

I sat quietly, my eyes locked on the speaker, but my mind was racing. This was a fairly new case? I'd assumed Anna had been confined to a wheelchair all her life.

The coordinator explained that Anna had fallen ill with a virus over the summer. When she didn't get better, her parents had taken her to the hospital, where meningitis and West Nile were ruled out. Eventually, she was diagnosed with post viral cerebellar ataxia, an inflammation of the cerebellum. This caused her clumsy body movements, inability to walk, headaches, nausea, and difficulty breathing and speaking. In just a week, her life had taken a direction she could never have imagined. I already admired Anna's persistence and strength—she seemed to welcome every challenge as though she lived by the quote, "What does not kill you makes you stronger"—but now I recognized an entirely new element to her greatness. Her smile, her work ethic, and her natural ability to make the best of her situation were not learned traits that came from years of living in a wheelchair. Instead, they were an outgrowth of her personality. Perhaps they were even a gift from God.

Anna continuously left the classroom for doctors' appointments and physical therapy. At one point, I only saw her two to three times a week for an hour at a time. To keep her from falling behind, I spent our time together covering the most important math topics and weekly strategies that would be essential to her success on the end-of-the-year exam.

Although Anna did not complete as many problems as her classmates, the problems she did finish were usually correct. Her questions to further her understanding were inquisitive and gave me ideas on how to better teach the class as a whole. How much more could Anna impress me?

Fitting in While Sitting Out

Sitting still and not moving for long intervals is both painful and nearly impossible for children. I routinely practiced several exciting strategies to maintain my students' attention and ensure fresh minds could keep up with the pace. For example, between each lesson and subject change, I told my class, "Stand up, push your chairs in, and let's get fresh."

Then I instructed, "Stand on your left leg and grab your right leg from behind."

Or, "While standing on one foot, grab your neck with your hand and stretch it softly to the side. Your brain is working hard."

I might finish with, "We need to make sure all the signals from our brains can get to the rest of our body. Let's do this while skip counting by sevens. Ready, set, go!"

Before I met Anna, I never thought twice about how a fun and refreshing activity like this could be a problem, but now I questioned myself. Anna couldn't fully participate. Should I eliminate this routine so she wouldn't feel left out?

As we stretched that first day, I looked over at Anna and was reassured by her confident smile. She was actively participating when she could and clearly enjoyed watching her classmates. She laughed each time they stumbled.

I caught up with her after class. "Hey, Anna, great job today. You continue to impress me with your hard work and resilience."

She smiled and let out a small giggle, saying, "Thank...you."

I continued, "When we are doing activities such as stretches, do you enjoy it? I couldn't help but notice you giggling."

"I...do..." she responded.

"It's...a...break...from...school...work...and...we...get... to...laugh...and...play...You...are...the...best...teacher...I... have...ever...had."

Her response put an end to my worries. I decided to continue the stretches and continued asking her opinion on our classroom activities.

Anna enjoyed being my assistant, helping me decide what worked and what did not. Her reasoning was quite entertaining. One day, after I asked her opinion on holding a math lesson outside, she explained why it wouldn't work.

"He...jumps...around...in...class...like...he's...in...an... ant...pile...How...do...you...expect...him...to...listen...outside...when...there...are...so...many...distractions?...If... one...ant...comes...in...his...area...he...will...go...crazy."

I laughed out loud. Her portrayal of Antoine was accurate.

Music to My Ears

There's no such thing as a magic bullet when it comes to discipline. Personally, I enjoy incentives. What can students individually earn for great behavior, and what can the class as a whole earn for exceptional behavior?

The answer is music! I love music, you love music, and you'd better believe students love it. When my students show me they are being responsible, I play music over the classroom speakers as they work on their assignments. I start with Mozart's classical music. The lack of lyrics really helps the students focus during independent work, while Jack Johnson's and Bobby McFerrin's groovy beats work great during group projects. One of my favorite groups is the Vitamin String Quartet, a strings orchestra that covers popular songs such as Rihanna's "We Found Love" and Adele's "Someone Like You." Anna in particular liked to lip sing to Rihanna's "Diamonds" while simultaneously focusing on the math assignment in front of her.

The music complimented another classroom incentive I had for my students—being rewarded for good behavior with open blinds and a clear view out our windows at the front of our school. Although BB gun shots had created holes in our windows and the ceiling leaked every time it rained, the view out our windows was incredible. From one end of the classroom to the other, we had a full view of every visitor, squirrel, tree, dog, and elderly neighborhood resident strolling by.

By comparison, as I drove home past some of the nicest schools in town, I often thought they looked like prisons with their tiny windows and complete separation from the community at large.

After Anna completed her off-campus physical rehabilitation sessions, she would return to school for afternoon classes. Her mom's car would pull up to the sidewalk 25 yards from our classroom window. Mom would get out of the car, remove Anna's wheelchair from the trunk, and reassemble it, then Mom and sister would carefully lift Anna out of the vehicle and into her chair.

One day, something was different. My students had behaved well throughout the day, so the blinds were open. After some murmurs and a student whispering "Anna is here," I delivered a simple redirection and we were back to the task at hand.

I continued, "The four steps we follow in long division are abbreviated to DMSB. This means Dangerous Monkeys Steal Bananas." The class burst out laughing, and I continued.

"Divide, multiply, subtract, bring do..." In the middle of my instruction, before I could finish the sentence, my students were off the carpet and moving to the windows.

What could possibly be exciting enough to distract the entire class, including my best behaved students?

Of course, it was Anna. Holding her mom's hand, Anna was walking on her own. Step by step, she was defying the odds.

One step for the infection that tried to take her life. One step for the bully who laughed at her before asking what it felt like to not be able to run. One step for the support her family continuously gave her. One step for the milestone she had just reached. One step for the hundreds and perhaps thousands of people she would compel to greatness by her heroic journey.

The entire class began to clap and encourage Anna although she could not hear them through the glass.

"*Way to go!*"

"*Look, she's walking!*"

"*You're awesome, Anna!*"

"*Wow!*"

I was moved to tears by the joy my fourth graders showed. They recognized how amazing Anna's journey had been. She taught them lessons I could never teach.

Day by day, Anna continued to earn her motor skills back. She eventually began walking with a walker, and her writing speed and accuracy increased by more than 50%. The state exams did not pose a problem, and she passed each and every test. The only accommodation she received was assistance in writing a full-page essay.

I wrote Anna a short letter at the end of the year.

Anna,

It has been a pleasure having you in class this year. I am inspired by your hard work inside and outside the classroom! With your work ethic and friendly person-ality, I know you will be a success in whatever you do. Keep being great and never lose that smile on your face; it makes others happy too. Good luck!

Mr. Duncan

Anna's resilience inspired many of my short moral lessons the following year. I began implementing a moment of silence in which my students were required to stand quiet for 10 seconds with consequences if they disrupted their fellow classmates.

"Be thankful for what you have," I told them after we brain-stormed things they might have to be thankful for.

On another day, it might be, "Be thankful for your health. Appreciate the steps you took when you rolled out of bed this morning. You can walk!"

The next day, it might be, "Be happy you can see, hear, smell, taste, and touch. Take a few moments to appreciate something you saw, heard, smelled, tasted, or touched this morning."

Anna was inspirational. She offered lifelong lessons in how to deal cheerfully with adversity, giving her classmates a first-hand look at how to persevere in spite of the challenges that came their way. This was something they badly needed and with a little guidance from their teacher a lesson that was well received.

CHAPTER 6:

HIGHLY INTELLIGENT, DEEPLY ANGRY JOHN

There is no great genius without some touch of madness.

Aristotle

His smirk more confident than James Dean's, carrying a single plastic rose and a white envelope, John set the letter on Jessie's desk and placed the flower delicately on top.

I mean, what do you expect? He'd read the romantic series Twilight and engulfed himself in Katniss's soap opera with Gale and Peeta Malark in the amazing Hunger Games trilogy. He might have only been in the fourth grade, yet his academic tests were already placing him at a ninth grade reading level.

I remembered my fourth grade crush all too well. Her name was Cadence. She was always smiling and looking at me. It scared me to death! There was no way in the world I could let her know I liked her. It would have been the end of life as I knew it.

I survived all of fourth grade without anyone knowing my greatest secret, but fifth grade was a different story.

"Class time!" Mr. Thomas, my first male teacher, screamed at the top of his lungs. Recess was over, and it was time to get back to learning. I was running to be first in line and was abruptly stopped by two girls who jumped in my way, causing me to take Robert Frost's "path less chosen" to avoid running them over like bowling pins.

"Joshua, we need to tell you something."

Play it cool, play it cool, I thought to myself. *Cadence is right here. Don't do anything to let her know she makes me feel like a great monarch migration is happening inside my chest.*

"Josh, who do you like?" the girls creepily asked in unison. It reminded me of the two little girls riding down the hallway on their tricycles in the horror thriller *The Shining*.

Samantha went first. "Do you like me?"

Cadence asked, "Or do you like me?"

How could this be happening? One second I was king of the basketball court, dribbling and weaving through my friends' defense to score the winning bucket, and the next I was blind-sided with a question involving my secret crush.

"Umm, umm, what do you mean?" I hoped this deviant answer would buy me some time.

"Answer the question, Josh. You have to like one of us!" Melanie exclaimed.

Dang! These girls were good.

"I like…" My head moved back and forth like a bobble head. "I like… Samantha!"

Samantha's eyes lit up like the New York City skyline on New Year's Eve while Cadence's heart sank. I could tell by the way her beautiful almond-shaped brown eyes fell to the ground.

What had I done? Had this really just happened? I was so scared the girl I liked would know I had feelings for her that I panicked and told her friend she was the one I liked?

Samantha bought me a ring and wanted to hold hands every time she saw me. After a week, I buried the ring in the sand, told her I'd lost it, and vowed to never speak again.

I was exceedingly nervous when it came to "crushes" and talking to girls in class, but John never hesitated, not for a second.

The Challenge

Spider-Man once said, "With great power comes great responsibility. This is my gift, my curse."

My greatest challenge this particular year was helping John recognize his great responsibility. Of necessity, this also meant recognizing his curse.

John never shied away from any situation, and almost every student looked up to him because of his natural gifts, but he was frequently angry.

One particular morning remains fresh in my memory. When the 7:45 bell rang, it was time to pick up my students from the cafeteria where they were finishing breakfast. All the students were loud and struggling to follow normal rules and procedures.

Teachers tell stories of how a full moon or change of weather drastically increases misbehavior throughout the school, and this was one of those days. Students were running in the hall, objects kept flying across the room, and voice levels remained too loud. John kept raising his hand for my attention, so I told him I'd speak to him after I finished taking attendance.

Two minutes later, I heard a scream of desperation. I turned to see John breaking pencil after pencil in an all-out rage. I shouted his name to get his attention, but it was too late. Blood flowing from his lower wrist down the outside of his hand and past the pinky joined a growing puddle on the floor. In his dangerous emotional state, he'd stabbed himself.

"John, what have you done?" I asked in disappointment.

"I had my hand raised and you wouldn't come to me. You ignored me!" he replied angrily.

"You're telling me that because I couldn't get to you in two minutes, you went and did something like this? You didn't even express an emergency!" I looked him directly in the eyes. "I believed in you. I still believe in you. When all those other teachers were telling me stories about you, I told them I didn't want to hear it. I'm not mad at you, John. I'm disappointed."

The emotion I felt turned to moisture in my eyes like spring's first shower, and John recognized it.

Anger Is Sadness's Bodyguard

My disappointment was clear. There wasn't any room or need for anger.

I sent John to the nurse to be cleaned up. A janitor came to our classroom and mopped up the blood. John's family was notified that he'd be spending the remainder of the day in the office until they could pick him up.

With great power comes great responsibility, and John had more power than he knew what to do with. His feelings ran deep. His parent's imminent divorce haunted him. His advanced mind continually raced, seeking answers, asking questions such as, "Why did I end up with my dad while my sister moved with my mom?" He noticed people responded to him when he spoke. He realized his presence resulted in an audience even when he wasn't trying to impress anyone.

He once told me, "I never asked to be followed."

I replied, "Exactly. That means you're a natural leader. If people are going to follow you, wouldn't you rather lead them down a great path as opposed to a bad one?"

The weight on his shoulders was heavy, and I only had a year to turn his life around. How could I help him learn to control his emotions and thoughts instead of letting his emotions and thoughts control him?

I recalled how, as the new school year began, chatter had floated around as teachers learned their new student rosters. Certain students were always the object of gossip. These were usually kids like John who demanded so much energy that stories about them circulated before they even entered the classroom.

This particular year, before anything incriminating could be shared, I'd approached these teachers and said, "I want to go into the new year with a clean slate. The students are all the same to me as I am to them. Perhaps I can come to you later in the year for advice."

I sought out this much-needed advice sooner than I expected. One day early in the school year, John was laughing with other students in the cafeteria. His crush was sitting right next to him. She reached over and playfully tapped his cheek, and John reached over and slapped her. He said he meant for it to be soft, but it wasn't even close to soft. The red mark on her face caused tears to stream from her eyes. I took him to the office where he was quickly suspended for three days. There wasn't any doubt: I would need a full support team to get John where he needed to be.

His teacher from the previous year was someone I admired. She was passionate about her students' success, and her words of encouragement were inspiring, so I told her what had happened in the cafeteria and also shared the story of John jabbing himself with a pencil.

She shook her head as if to say, "I'm glad someone understands what I've gone through."

We conversed for a solid 45 minutes. When she told me how John had once taken a sharp object and sliced his wrists until they bled, I cringed.

Her last story was the most frightening. She told of a time John abruptly stood up in the middle of a lesson, walked over to the window, opened it, and stood on the ledge, threatening to jump.

I was at a loss for words. John's few incidents in my classroom didn't compare to these stories.

Her advice was good. She told me to look for clues. The color of his eyes would change and he would ball up his fists before an outburst began. If I jumped in quickly, I could avoid whatever was about to happen.

That night, I couldn't stop thinking about John. What if he'd slipped when he'd hung over the edge? What if one of the cuts had hit a vein and he'd bled out? How would other students have felt if they'd seen their classmate fall from such a great height? What if something horrible happened on my watch? How could I live with it?

I was ready to give this student my all. I also knew my efforts could be for nothing if he made one really bad decision.

Baby Steps

I believe people are good at heart. We are not born to hate, hurt, or strike fear into others. Knowing this encouraged me to continue to work with John to control his outbursts and to try to figure out what was at the root of his anger.

When he wasn't angry, John's open-book personality made him a joy to be around. He didn't mind talking honestly about himself. If I could understand his thought processes, I decided, I could help him make better decisions.

As his classmates went to P.E. one day, I pulled John to the side.

"I'm going to ask you some questions," I told him, "but I want you to understand that you don't have to share anything you don't want to."

John began moving back and forth with his glasses on his nose and his hands crossed behind his back. His smile and body language suggested he was excited to share his thoughts.

I started with, "I'm curious, John. You are such an incredible scholar and person. You make all A's, and you're popular among your friends. At the same time, I've seen you try to hurt yourself. Other teachers have shared stories about your past with me. I've seen you get enraged and out of control. What is happening in that wonderful mind of yours?"

John looked me directly in the eyes, slightly popped his neck forward, raised his eyebrows, and began to circle his finger next to the side of his head.

"What do you mean?" I asked. It looked like he was signaling that he was crazy, yet I didn't want to put words in his mouth or ideas in his head.

"You know...Crazy." He placed his hands by his side and waited quietly.

"Something is crazy?"

He shook his head back and forth.

"You're crazy?" I asked with a look of discernment.

He began to nod.

I didn't think John had a mental illness, so I said, "You are not crazy, my friend! You are amazing! You have the ability to make everyone around you happy, and I'm so proud of you, just as so many people are in your life, but if you're going to tell me you're crazy, I want to know why you think that!"

John began sharing. His mom, dad, and grandpa had all been in prison at one time, and his mom was still in prison. His dad and stepmom were in the middle of a divorce. He told me he and his dad often argued about small things and that he felt uncomfortable and angry.

After hearing his story, we talked about making good choices even in heartbreaking situations. I shared some of my past with him, one on one. I told him about good choices I'd made even when it was tough to make them. I gave him specific examples.

After that day, slowly but surely, John's behavior began to change. I understood what he was going through, I cared, and I had asked him to try to handle his emotions more positively. He had needed someone to understand, to give him some time, and to give him constructive alternatives to his usual behavior.

After some time passed, I decided to share some of my story with my class. It had helped John, and he wasn't the only struggling student in my room; he was just the most volatile. I told the quiet class how my mom hadn't made good decisions and had died at a relatively young age. When I finished, I asked my students to look at me.

"Do you think I'm successful?" I asked them. "Do I smile every day? Have I gained so many amazing friends that I can no longer keep count? Do I continue to get better and help others around me become the best they can be? Or did I make the same bad decisions my mom made? Did I follow her path to trouble and unhappiness?" After a brief discussion, I concluded, "Always remember, no matter what the situation is, you have a choice as to who you will become!"

John abruptly got up and began walking towards me. I had just shared something extremely dear to my heart, and he was walking up to give me a hug with the strength of a boa constrictor. He whispered, "You are an awesome person, Mr. Duncan."

His empathy was one of the many great gifts John possessed. He had an innate ability to relate to others sincerely, especially those in need. In a classroom of 25 students, someone is always sad about something or having trouble at home, and John was always quick to give condolences to his classmates. He could sense when his peers were in need, and he did what he could to make them smile. His hug meant the world to me.

Later that day, I asked him to wait after class and to think about something for me. "For so long," I told him, "I haven't had a problem with you. We are having fewer incidents, and you seem like a completely different person. Why do you think this is? What can you attribute your great behavior to?"

His response was golden.

"I'm learning about the power of choice," he responded. "I have a decision to make in every situation, and I'm making good ones."

My primary focus was to help John embrace his greatest attributes and use them to help the people following him be better than they were before. Day by day, I worked to build John's leadership qualities instead of dwelling on his negative behavior.

Nonetheless, common rules and procedures such as raising your hand before you talk, not interrupting the instructor, and controlling the volume of your voice at library time created friction. Environments where he was required to follow rules were not his forte.

I explained, "If it were up to me, I wouldn't care how loud you were! You are one of the smartest kids in my class and can get all your work done even when talking. But what about the friends who are watching you? What if you do extremely well on your tests because you're naturally gifted but then the people you are distracting fail because they've been paying attention to you instead of what I'm teaching? Is this going to make them feel happy and successful? Let's not think only about ourselves; let's also think about our friends."

John nodded and replied, "That makes sense."

I would have to remind him thousands of times during the year not to distract others, and it took a lot of self-control for me to be patient. If an employee doesn't follow the rules, a boss can fire them, but it's not as easy to fire a student.

One day I explained, "If my boss walks around the corner and you're jumping up and down and using a loud voice in the hallway, are you the only one who gets in trouble?"

John shook his head, pointing his finger, reminding me of the famous E.T. scene.

I nodded. "I'll get in trouble too, and I need my job to pay for my car and apartment. I need my job to feed myself and support my family! Can you please help me out next time around?"

Once again, instead of focusing on what he'd done wrong, I took the time to explain what a better alternative looked like. Soon, that funny smirk was covering his face. He was beginning to realize we were on the same team.

Perspective

Try to put yourself in John's shoes. Imagine you're a troubled child having issues at home beyond your control. Not knowing how to manage them, you act out in school. This natural response leads to stressed and overworked teachers becoming frustrated. Since patience has fallen short, they shout their demands, and there isn't time to explain the why's and why not's. How can a teacher find the time to explain better options to a student when every other student in the classroom needs every available second to get ready for exams? Rarely do these students have teachers who can relate to them without losing their composure.

Imagine what years of frustration emanating from the adults around you can do to the mind and spirit of a child. Yes, we teachers face great pressures, but we also occasionally forget we are the adults. As a helpful reminder, I posted phrases on my desk such as, "I am the adult and these are my students. I am their role model in every situation. I will always set my standards high. No excuses allowed."

It is our job to show students how to act in times of tribulation. We need to remain calm, complacent, and in control of our actions. When we scream and yell, we show our students we do not have control over our own emotions and actions. At this point, how can a teacher expect students to have control over theirs?

I wanted to make sure I was a leader for John. Through some sort of miracle, I never once yelled at him (I'm not counting the time I shouted to stop him from breaking more pencils), and John's greatness continued to present itself. In science class, he displayed his keen understanding of spiders, creatures most of us know little about and fear, including yours truly.

Before any friends or family members tell you, I'll go ahead and spill the beans: I'm afraid of spiders.

I once took a beautiful woman out on a date. We went hiking and even packed a lunch and blanket for picnicking. The sun was setting and the ambiance was perfect. On our way back to the car, I decided to take a last-minute shortcut. Leaving the winding paved path, I led us down the road less traveled and through a few trees. I told my date, "It's a shortcut! Follow me!" I could tell she was hesitant, but my confidence was reassuring, so she followed me. As I gallantly held a tree branch aside so she could pass through, I suddenly heard a girl scream.

"Ahhhhhh!"

When my date began laughing hysterically along with the biker riding by, I suddenly realized the high-pitched plea for help had come from me. Hanging from one of the last branches was a nickel-sized spider staring me straight in the eyes as if to say, "Not coming this way!"

I understand that I'm only afraid of spiders because I know so little about them. If I took the time to study the species, I would realize most spiders aren't harmful. Instead, fear takes over and all spiders in my path receive a death sentence. John took the time to read books about spiders so he wasn't afraid, but he was an anomaly.

One day as recess was ending, I heard a group of girls simultaneously shout. If you've never heard a group of elementary girls scream, believe me when I say it's one of the loudest noises known to mankind. I quickly walked over to see what all the fuss was about.

"What's going on, ladies?"

All fingers pointed to John.

Lost in his own world, bending his head to the left and twisting his hand back around to view the top again, John was watching a spider move from the top of his hand to his palm.

The girls and I thought this was creepy. Wasn't it going to eat him alive? Wasn't his hand going to fall off from a poisonous bite?

To John, the spider wasn't a threat; it was just a new friend. Once again, I was the one learning a lesson. I needed to learn more about what I knew nothing about. I no longer wanted to make the mistake of fearing something harmless.

So many times, discrimination results from a lack of knowledge, curiosity, and a willingness to learn, whether it's about something like a spider or about other people's beliefs and cultures. Fearing what we do not know leads to terrible prejudices.

Nonetheless, I have to admit, I was extremely frightened the day it wasn't a spider in John's hand but a live scorpion. I asked him to immediately put it down. With his trademark smirk and a look of pure confidence, he bent down and let the scorpion crawl into the dirt. Sure enough, the scorpion hesitated a few seconds and then scurried away without using its stinger.

Thinking of Others, Learning to Care

John's ability to comprehend higher level thinking allowed me to use his mistakes as learning opportunities. One day while walking through the hallway, John was having trouble staying in line with the rest of his class. After numerous reminders to get back in line, something happened. John reached out to quickly snatch his friend's glasses and accidentally bent the frames. Oblivious of the ramifications, he laughed.

I asked the other student if he was okay and assessed the damage. Then I spoke to John.

"Why would you grab something so delicate with such carelessness?" I was careful to keep my tone curious rather than angry. "How much do you think those glasses cost?"

John responded, "I don't know. I wasn't trying to break them. And he probably has insurance anyways."

"Insurance huh…And what exactly is insurance?" I allowed a trace of sarcasm to enter my voice. I had a feeling John didn't understand how insurance worked, and I wanted to get his attention.

"It means he'll just get some new ones for free."

His response confirmed my assumption. I responded, "You're telling me he can get his glasses fixed for free if you break them? If that's the case, why wouldn't everybody break their glasses when they need new ones?"

John shrugged.

I continued, "If your family purchases a brand new home in southern California and it burns down in a wildfire, will you get a new house for free?" I shook my head no. "That isn't how it works. Your friend has to pay money towards insurance in order to qualify for a new pair of glasses. Your family would have to purchase thousands of dollars in insurance on the house before anyone would help you rebuild. Insurance isn't free. Your friend's glasses are fragile and cost money. Money that his family could use on food instead of having to fix something another student broke. I know you didn't break them on purpose, but you should care that they're broken."

I respected John's ability to learn. Although his continuous disregard for common rules and procedures was frustrating, he rarely made a serious mistake twice, and his maturity continued to grow throughout the year.

I called him to my desk one day and said, "I need your help, John."

He looked at me as if I were crazy and then changed his posture to a raised chest and a smile.

"What can I help with?" he asked in anticipation.

"I'm not sure what to do with Hannah," I confided. "She won't stop whistling in class. She also won't stop talking above the lecture, and her distractions are making it hard to do my job. I was having some trouble with you earlier in the year, and now you're doing great. I thought maybe you could give me some advice on how to make her stop whistling?"

"Hmm." He grabbed his chin and stood there thinking. "Let me work with her," he said after a moment. "Sometimes when you tell her to do something, she does the opposite."

I responded, "All right, give it a shot."

A few minutes later, I noticed John quietly talking to Hannah out of the corner of my eye. When he finished, I began the next lesson. Ten minutes passed, and I couldn't believe what I was observing. Hannah hadn't said a word! Somehow, after a few short minutes, John had patched up a problem I'd spent the entire year working on.

From that point on, I allowed these two highly intelligent students to work with one another, and the results were brilliant. They motivated one another academically while simultaneously cancelling out each other's negative behavior. Hmmm. Sometimes two negatives really can make a positive!

After putting so much energy into developing John's strengths, it was a pleasure to finally get to meet his dad and stepmom. As we shared stories of success and struggle, I could tell his parents loved John with all their hearts. They mentioned how he had been emotionally guarded previously but had recently begun to open up. I told them how he consistently gave me hugs at the end of each day. They smiled and his dad responded, "He really looks up to you."

These are the moments teachers flash a smile and simply say thank you. They might look as though nothing momentous has just occurred, but on the inside, they feel a world of emotions. I had spent a year of aches and pains, smiles and laughs, sweat and tears to try to ensure John developed into the amazing man he had the potential to be. Hearing those words made it all worthwhile.

The Last Day of School

When the last bell of the school year rang, the moment every student and teacher looks forward to arrived. It was summertime!

At that, my greatest challenge of the year threw me a curve ball. No hug, no goodbye wave, not even a farewell grunt as John sprinted from the back of the classroom, stumbled over a backpack, and knocked a fellow classmate into the wall. Before I could call his name, he was gone. Instead of chasing him down the hallway, I made sure the other students all received proper farewells.

Why had John run? Was he overwhelmed with emotion he didn't know how to handle? Did he want to find Jessie to give her one last rose? Of course, it was only fitting that he would do this on the last day of school after so many days of progress and countless hours of growth. I smiled to myself and brushed it off.

A few months later, John was back at school, in the fifth grade. Twelve weeks into the year, I ran into him in the hallway. He was walking slowly behind his class with his fists clenched, his face as red as a cape held by a Spanish matador. He was clearly angry, but he was just as clearly keeping himself in check. I asked his teacher if I could pull him to the side and catch up with him a bit, and she obliged.

"I'm proud of you, John! Do you know why?" I asked.

"No." He looked at me with curiosity and a slight change in his expression.

"I don't even know what happened to make you angry, but I love how you separated yourself from the situation. You have learned to control your emotions instead of letting them control you! You did not make a bad decision in the hallway! That is pretty awesome of you."

I didn't ask for details. I wanted to compliment him and avoid giving power to the negativity. Instead of going to P.E. with the rest of his class, John helped me rearrange my room for the upcoming week so we could continue to talk.

"How are your parents?" I asked. "Do you still see your dad on the weekends?"

His response was the best thing I could have heard. "Actually, no, everything is different now."

I continued placing fraction blocks into separate baggies in preparation for Monday's lesson while he said, "They're back together now! They needed a break, and now they're making it work!"

"That sounds amazing!" I responded.

"We had to get rid of our two dogs, though," John told me. "They wouldn't stop peeing on the tile! Plus they needed a new home where they wouldn't be stuck inside the house all the time."

He proceeded to tell me how well his year was going and how he had not gotten in trouble once so far. Sure enough, he had learned the most important lesson: life decisions do not make you, but you make life decisions. He was developing the ability to understand the power of choice. He was beginning to understand that he was the author of his very own story, and he was just beginning to write his story. John was now equipped with the tools to conquer life's obstacles with confidence.

I expect this young man to do great things when he fully matures. If he reminds you of any of your students, I hope you will challenge them to be great instead of focusing on their negatives. You could be the teacher who turns their world around.

CHAPTER 7:

IF NOT ME, THEN WHO?

The only thing worse than being blind is having sight but no vision.

Hellen Keller

At a small Subway table for two, the clear white cup of water slid from hand to hand as condensation dripped down the ridged sides. The restaurant was on the fourth floor of the beautiful North Dallas mall overlooking the city's finest skating rink. Nervousness lurked in the air.

She inadvertently pushed what was left of her flaky red nail polish completely up to her cuticles while children laughed, fell on the ice, and followed the instructions of their figure skating coach below.

I looked forward, and our eyes met.

She told me, "I love you so much, but I'm afraid of this doubt. It's always in the back of my mind, and I don't know if it will ever leave. How could we ever have a child? I want to have four children, live comfortably, eat out, travel, and not have to worry. How could we do this on your salary given the school loans you still owe? I know I sound like such a bad person."

I battled back, "I'm young, sweetheart. Believe in me. I'm driven. I want the same things you do. I wouldn't be with you if I didn't, but it takes time." I continued, "Would you choose these financial comforts over being with someone you're compatible with?"

I kept talking. "I hope to live to be 80, 90, or even 100. That's 60 to 80 more years." I counted out loud, "One year, two years, three years, 10 years, 15 years, 20 years, 30 years, 40 years, half a century, 60 years, 70 years…Wow, that is an incredibly long time. If you choose to be with someone for the rest of your life, I pray to God he inspires every atom in your body. I hope he can always make you smile. I hope he has enough love for you to rub your feet when they ache, hold the door for you, and kiss your forehead, not just in the infatuation stage but for the rest of your life. I pray he believes in you and doesn't want to change you. True love is when someone compliments who you are and you compliment them just the same."

She didn't say anything, so I added, "Money is important; I understand that. Believe me, believe in me, and wait on me. We can and will live comfortably."

Her beautiful brown eyes hadn't moved. I could tell she was lost in her own world, a world of thoughts and feelings and doubts.

She paused and then began to speak. "I do believe in you; it's just that…I'm getting older! I don't have any children of my own. What do I have to show for myself?"

I responded, "Honey, just because you don't have a child like all your other friends doesn't mean you aren't a success. You have a beautiful life, and you impact every person who sees your amazing smile. There's no need to rush; you have plenty of time to create your own path and have children of your own! Just wait until we're ready."

She still looked unconvinced, so I told her, "I know you're ready for something in life that I can't provide right now. If you feel you have to have it right this second, then you have my complete support. Just know this: you have time. We are great together, and we will only get better. I promise you, we will live comfortably, but it takes time. Wait for me, believe in me, but if you can't, I understand."

She nodded and we both silently accepted that what needed to be said had been said. I reached out, took her small soft hands, and slid them into mine, my thumbs on top of her petite wrists.

I kissed both of her hands. "I know that teaching isn't the highest paying job. I know I'm not living in the biggest house or driving the nicest car."

She quickly interrupted me. "That's not what matters to me, Josh."

I continued, "But if not me, then who? If not me, then who is going to be there to help these children succeed? Who is going to inspire the boy or girl who doesn't have a father figure at home? Or even worse, the dad is home but addicted to drugs, foul language, and negativity?

"Who is going to teach these children that men and women can walk strong, morally sound paths?

"Who else is blessed enough to have survived the struggle of being raised with their grandparents, jumping from home to home because four of his six immediate family members were incarcerated?

"Who will tell the crying child that she's incredible, that she's uniquely one in billions, that there isn't another human being in the history of mankind exactly like her?

"Who will tell these kids it doesn't matter what life throws at them, that they have a choice to succeed, a choice to chase dreams, and a choice to be as great as they desire?

"Who will have the audacity to endow the impoverished child, the same child the rest of the world overlooks, with expectations of greatness?

"That's why I do it," I told her. "If not me, then who?"

I believe that two hearts can grow together if they are invested in one another and the investment is love, not money, but she couldn't overcome her doubts, and life moved on.

Living Up to Expectations

Another relationship and I was dating a girl who had recently been laid off from a start-up company. This was her first job since graduating college, and losing it really hurt her confidence. We sat down and contemplated her next steps.

I softly said, "This isn't the end of the world. You are young, beautiful, and have a degree from a great university. You have working experience on your resume. The city is booming, and thousands of jobs are available."

Together, we started researching marketing positions aligned with her qualifications. We updated her resume and found local meet-ups where professionals young and old could socialize, network, and share ideas over appetizers and drinks. We attended a meet-up together, and I spoke about my ambitions to create educational tablet applications and market them to school districts across the nation. Like me, each person I met spoke passionately about his or her ideas.

As we left the event hand in hand, we began to talk.

"I think that went well; how about you?" I asked.

A glance at her told me my feelings weren't reciprocated.

"It went okay," she said.

"You did great," I encouraged her. "You met a lot of generous individuals who could use someone like you to pump out social media. Don't worry. A job, an awesome job, is out there."

She responded, "It's not that."

By now, we were at my car, so I opened her door, held her hand, and helped her into the passenger seat, assuring her stability in the elegant black heels she wore.

Walking around the car, I wondered what was bothering her. Soon, the car was in gear, and so was my attention. "Well, what is it?"

"Remember the elderly man I was speaking with?" she asked.

"I sure do; he seemed like a nice guy."

"Well, he was at first, but then he said something upsetting." She paused a moment. "He said something about you, Josh! He said I should drop you and date one of the more successful men there."

Wow. I felt betrayed. Someone who had smiled when he shook my hand, looked me straight in the eye, and told me I had chosen a very honorable profession had minutes later said something this harsh.

I responded, "Of course he's going to say that; you're beautiful, and he doesn't understand why I teach or how important it is."

She added fuel to the fire. "Josh, my dad said the same thing."

My students' successes, the smiles on their faces, were being questioned because of concerns about money. A businessman told my girlfriend I didn't deserve her and her father questioned her decision because her boyfriend, a teacher, didn't make a lucrative salary.

Never Give In

The pressure to make big money sickens me and the fact that teachers do not make big money sickens me even more. Teachers face this pressure every day. Instead of folding, they remind themselves that they're in it to change the world.

Teachers make a difference by producing lawyers, doctors, engineers, and men and women who go into business. Teachers plant the seeds of success in every great profession. Teachers are the spark that starts the fire. Teachers apply the pressure to coal that makes diamonds. Teachers play a critical role in ensuring each one of their students becomes a productive citizen.

Years ago, Taylor Mali, a teacher, author and speaker wrote a poem titled "What Teachers Make."

He says the problem with teachers is, "What is a kid going to learn from someone who decided his best option in life was to become a teacher?"

He reminds the other dinner guests that it's true what they say about teachers: those who can, do; those who can't, teach.

*I decide to bite my tongue instead of his
and resist the temptation to remind the other dinner guests
that it's also true what they say about lawyers.*

Because we're eating, after all, and this is polite company.

*"I mean, you're a teacher, Taylor," he says.
"Be honest. What do you make?"*

*And I wish he hadn't done that
(asked me to be honest)
because, you see, I have a policy
about honesty and ass-kicking:
if you ask for it, I have to let you have it.*

You want to know what I make?

*I make kids work harder than they ever thought they could.
I can make a C+ feel like a Congressional medal of honor
and an A- feel like a slap in the face.
How dare you waste my time with anything less than your
very best.*

I make kids sit through 40 minutes of study hall
in absolute silence. No, you may not work in groups.
No, you may not ask a question.
Why won't I let you get a drink of water?
Because you're not thirsty, you're bored, that's why.

I make parents tremble in fear when I call home:
I hope I haven't called at a bad time,
I just wanted to talk to you about something Billy said today.
Billy said, "Leave the kid alone. I still cry sometimes,
don't you?"
And it was the noblest act of courage I have ever seen.

I make parents see their children for who they are
and what they can be.

You want to know what I make?

I make kids wonder,
I make them question.
I make them criticize.
I make them apologize and mean it.
I make them write, write, write.
And then I make them read.
I make them spell definitely beautiful, definitely beautiful,
definitely beautiful over and over
and over again until they will never misspell
either one of those words again.
I make them show all their work in math.
And hide it on their final drafts in English.
I make them understand that if you got this (brains)
then you follow this (heart) and if someone ever
tries to judge you by what you make,
you give them this (the finger).

Let me break it down for you, so you know what I say is true:
I make a gosh-damn difference! What about you?

The trials and tribulations teachers face are countless, but so are the opportunities. Teachers know our impact on the world is too valuable to sacrifice. Eric Thomas, a motivational speaker and the great mind behind the book *The Secret to Success*, once stated, "The most important thing is this: to be able at any moment to sacrifice what you are for who you will become."

I knew I was on the right path, and with every ounce of my soul I was proud to make a positive difference in the lives of my young students. Indeed, I was making more of a difference than could be measured by currency.

CHAPTER 8:

A CLOSE-UP LOOK
AT POVERTY

In a country well governed, poverty is something to be ashamed of.

In a country badly governed, wealth is something to be ashamed of.

Confucius

The stench reminded me of sickness. I wasn't sure if it was the residue of previously cooked meat still stuck on the pan or just the hamburger itself cooked without seasoning.

The words "Come get your food" meant we'd better scramble to the table if we wanted to avoid trouble. I was seven years old, and at this point in life, my dad had his own place. My uncle was living with us, and though he wasn't much of a cook, he demanded that we eat every last bite of his horrid smelling, seasoning lacking, low-grade hamburger meat before we were allowed to leave the table.

To this day, I am thankful we had a dog in the house. Looking at my uncle out of the corner of my eye, I would simultaneously dig a fork into the garbage of a meal with one hand while my other hand delivered piece after piece to my canine friend waiting anxiously at my feet.

What did I eat at home? For about a year straight, beans, which were always served with the meat. My only other source of nutrition came from the meals I received when school was in session.

As a young child, I convinced myself I was a special type of vegetarian. The "special" came from the fact that I hated the meat we ate at home but somehow I felt differently about burgers from McDonald's.

During this period, I met a strange man. My uncle often kept to himself, typically staying in his room or sitting on the porch. My dad was usually either working or with my uncle. My brothers always left the house on ventures of their own, so little old me was free to roam the world.

Behind our house was a bayou and a large section of woods. Each day, I took a walk around town but was careful to return home before sunset. No one asked me to be home before sunset; I came because I had to walk through the woods to get home again, and I was afraid of the dark..

On weekends, I awakened early and left the bed I shared with my brothers to begin my daily journey. One particular morning was a little different. Only five minutes away from our house and into the woods, I noticed an older man in his fifties or sixties. He was sitting on a stump and had his few possessions stored in a local grocery cart easily distinguished by its colors. Next to him were two boxes filled with an assortment of donuts.

Even at a young age, I had developed a strong sense of how to avoid danger. I recall my vivid step-by-step imagination of what I'd do if he tried to grab me. I would kick him and run. That old man wouldn't catch me!

"Hey, son, are you hungry?" The man started the conversation.

"What do you have?" I responded curiously.

As soon as he showed me the open box of donuts, I couldn't help but indulge my sweet tooth. The man didn't say much and only answered my questions as I asked him, "How long is your beard?" and "Where do you live?" and "Where is your family?"

Later that week, I told one of my brothers about the donuts and the man I'd met.

"Are you kidding me?" he asked. "You ate donuts from a bum. He dug them out of the trash."

My brother was quick to tell me how gross I was and that I should stay away from the man. In hindsight, I don't blame him. A young child alone with a stranger sounds frightening.

Nonetheless, the next weekend, I was right back with my friend in the woods, asking questions.

"Did you get these donuts out of the trash? That's what my big brother said!"

To my satisfaction, he told me he went by the donut shop each evening before it closed and the workers gave him the remaining donuts. If they didn't give them away, it was store policy to throw them away.

I enjoyed a delicious breakfast each weekend and always knew I'd have food to eat, even if it was sometimes unpalatable, but some children truly don't know where their next meal is going to come from.

When I started teaching in a lower income public school system that provided free breakfast and free lunch, I was initially bewildered to see students taking extra food. Sometimes they stuffed open burritos in their pockets or packs of microwaved pancakes in their backpacks.

Soon, I realized that every one of these "hoarding" students was from a poor family. Their clothes were tattered and they had dark rings under their eyes.

My class began saving all our extra food for select students in need of nutrition, especially items they could take home to eat. Our school even started a program to send home large bags of snacks and non-perishable items. Nonetheless, food anxiety remained a real issue for many of my students.

A Bed to Sleep In

Besides food anxiety, here's a typical and horrifying story of what lower income kids have to deal with.

A meeting was scheduled for one of my students who was on a streak of acting out and falling asleep in class. Our principal and assistant principal were attending the meeting along with the student's father. The mother was a drug addict who'd been in prison since giving birth to her child, my student. As often happens, she'd passed the addiction along to her baby, so doses of this student's medication contained narcotics. A couple of weeks earlier, we learned at the meeting, the narcotic doses had been completely stopped and new medicines were being prescribed.

During the meeting, the child's father told us his daughter, my student, had been staying with her grandparents because he worked evenings. The grandparents had failed to tell him until the day before the meeting that they'd been evicted, resulting in the three of them sleeping in their truck throughout the cold night without heat. They claimed they were too embarrassed to tell him and didn't want to lose the privilege of caring for their granddaughter.

The dad assured us that he would house his parents and daughter until they could get back on their feet. The administration and I collaborated to create a plan to help his daughter make it through the next stages of becoming a normal little girl.

I was always blessed with a bed to sleep in, although sometimes I had to share it with my three brothers. At such a young age, I didn't mind having to share. It brought me warmth and security from the dark until the sun rose the next day.

The continuous battle my students faced gave the battle I'd faced during my childhood greater purpose. I could share with them how I'd once been in a similar boat. The good news was that my boat had made it through the storm. The teacher they looked up to had once been a struggling child just like them. If I could make it, they could make it, too.

Could You Walk a Mile in Their Shoes?

Although my grandparents were poor, I was the happiest kid on the planet. Every other evening, my grandma and I would watch the Houston Rockets play on TV. She wasn't as interested as I was, but she enjoyed listening to the game while she dove into her crosswords, puzzles, and card games. Soon, I began to eat, breathe, and speak the game of basketball.

One day, my grandpa surprised me with a basketball rim and backboard he'd collected from trash piles around the neighborhood. Although the rim and backboard were two different brands, I didn't care. He pulled out the tape measure and used chalk to mark the official 10-foot height on the tree and then drilled and bolted the backboard and rim into place.

In less than an hour, I was dribbling my first basketball and shooting my first baskets. A mere two weeks later, the once luscious green grass around the tree was a section of dirt. Any semblance of life had been pounded into oblivion by a boy with a basketball. I envisioned myself playing in the NBA as I practiced move after move. Something about the challenge of becoming better and showcasing my skills in front of a crowd made my blood flow faster and my soul come alive.

I had one pair of shoes. Given my adult size of 6'6, you can imagine the rate at which I grew as a kid. My toes were squeezing out of the torn and worn leather, and on numerous occasions, I accidentally scuffed the front of my shoe on the pavement and ripped off the outer layer of skin, bleeding all over the place. It didn't help that I naturally walked on my toes. New shoes were a necessity.

Grandma and Grandpa took me to look for shoes at the discount store Payless. Hakeem Olajuwon, one of my favorite players from the Houston Rockets, had recently released a shoe that was affordable to all, even my grandparents. I could not have been more excited to have my new Hakeem Olajuwon shoes! He was the best player for the Rockets, and I was thrilled and humbled to wear his signature shoe.

Years passed. I successfully competed in a number of competitive basketball leagues, but I never owned another pair of Hakeem Olajuwons. If I had, my teammates would have made fun of me. Luckily, as I aged, my aunt started taking my brothers and me shopping. She accepted the responsibility of putting clothes on our backs and shoes on our feet, and she allowed me to purchase the popular brands that fit the approval of my peers, but the value of my first pair of basketball shoes went beyond the price my grandparents paid for them. They were a gift when my love for basketball was beginning to bloom, and they allowed me to develop the confidence to excel among my peers. Maybe they weren't the most expensive shoes available, but they were new, and the only hole was the one I slid my foot into before I laced them up.

When a student of mine was finishing his last year of elementary school, I couldn't help but notice how worn his shoes were. The leather flapped up and down as if pleading with each and every step to be relieved of its duties. What made Sunni different from the other students who needed new shoes? Why did he remind me of myself?

Perhaps it was his story. As soon as he stepped into my classroom, I could tell he came from a poor family. His pants were sizes too short and his shirts were all faded. He always packed his own lunch, which ritually came with a small sandwich and chips. His lunch box was so tattered that the seams pulled away from the zipper.

In the classroom, poverty was never an excuse for Sunni or me. He participated in all activities and listened with the utmost attention. Although shy and still developing the courage to come out of his shell, he found ways to make his presence felt in a classroom of 20 strong-willed students. In spite of his hardships, poverty being the most blatant, Sunni succeeded academically.

Eventually, I learned that my friend Sunni and his family were immigrants from Pakistan. His dad was temporarily working in a different state for a telecommunications company, making just enough money to send home to feed his family. Sunni always spoke with a strong sense of gratefulness.

When I asked him why his family had moved from Pakistan, I heard a story I could never have anticipated.

"My uncle and father were two very popular people in the government," he told me. "Men blindfolded my uncle and shot him in the head. They were going to do the same to my father. This is why we moved here, Mr. Duncan. We took what little we had and escaped the country because our family was in danger."

It was hard to put myself in Sunni's shoes. I couldn't imagine the trauma his family had endured at the hands of an unstable government. We'd all heard "rags to riches" stories, but what about innocent children going from riches to rags? Sunni deserved a new pair of shoes.

I surprised him the same way my grandparents surprised me. A pair of durable Under Armours was slick enough to go along with his school uniform. I didn't want to give him the shoes in front of his peers and embarrass him, so one morning before the bell rang, I called him into my classroom and told him to sit down.

"I do not just run around giving things out," I told him. "I like to build self-sufficient people who can one day take care of themselves. That said, I decided to buy you a pair of shoes."

I opened up the pair of Under Armours in his size and handed him the box. He could not contain his excitement.

"In spite of your challenges, you have continued to be great," I told him. "You have succeeded in the classroom. You are kind and giving, and I know you are going to have a bright future. My only request is this: when you grow up and continue to be great, I ask that you pass along this gift to someone who deserves it."

Sunni slid on his shoes, thanked me, and gave me a huge hug. Who knew a pair of shoes could change a child's world the way it changed my world and Sunni's?

I'm not suggesting you go out and spend your paycheck on needy students, but I do encourage you, once or twice, to give a gift that can leave a lasting impact.

Emergencies and Medical Care

Growing up, I was closest to my brother Robert. He lived with me the most and never got in trouble. He went through an exciting stage during his mid teenage years. After purchasing a skateboard and learning how to ride it, Robert began riding skateboards around the city practicing tricks. Tagging along, I would occasionally jump on a skateboard when the other guys took breaks.

Within a day of learning the basics, I found myself gathering as much speed as I could to fly off a flight of five cement steps. Somehow, the injuries I sustained were never worse than a few bumps, scratches, and bruises. This is amazing, given that I was fearless.

I also suffered two swollen hands because sometimes childhood friends chase you with baseball bats. I lived through falling off houses into trees multiple times because sometimes I slipped when doing backflips off the roof. I received concussions because sometimes older brothers punch and push. I didn't need medical care for these injuries, but I had other issues that took me to the hospital.

From age nine to 17, stomach issues meant I went under the knife time after time. I vividly recall waking up nauseated from the anesthesia. Vomiting put stress on my fresh stitches, and the pressure caused the stitches to stretch. The surgery center smell will forever be imprinted on my senses.

Following the removal of two of my wisdom teeth, I was diagnosed with dry sockets and at one point cried through the intolerable pain. Again, my reaction to the anesthesia caused vomiting and led to infection of my sockets.

In addition, I had terrible cramps as a young child, something a lot of tall people have. The feeling can only be described as someone shredding each individual muscle in your leg. I would wiggle around and cry for hours instead of sleeping.

Through the pain, I was fortunate to have love. Grandpa's gentle-giant personality came with kindness.

"Grandpa," I would quietly whisper. For some reason, I was intensely anxious about scaring him. "Grandpa," a little bit louder this time.

"Yes, son." He would not move as he opened his eyes.

I would tell him my legs were cramping, and he would come massage my legs in the middle of the night until I felt better. He was able to help with my growing pains, but what happens when your parents, grandparents, or legal guardians don't have health insurance and you get sick or hurt?

One day, the pain started behind my eyes and wouldn't stop. It spread from the eye sockets to the side of my head while nausea targeted my chest and stomach.

After diagnosing my symptoms as migraines, Grandma gave me aspirin and put cold damp rags on my head and neck. Calling a doctor was out of the question as it meant spending hundreds of dollars. If we did that, we wouldn't be able to put food on the table. Even worse, we would miss out on our favorite pizza buffet Grandma and Grandpa took us to every other Friday evening.

That night, I woke up feeling abnormally sick. As soon as I stood up in an effort to reach the bathroom, sickness overtook me and I fell to the floor vomiting. I lay on the bedroom floor flat and motionless. Something was wrong. Rising to my knees, the sickness delivered more heavy punches. Once I reached the bathroom, all I could do was dry heave, a result of not having anything left in my stomach to vomit.

All home remedies were given and my temperature in the low hundreds was assessed every other hour, but my sickness did not go away. On the third day, Grandpa finally took me to the doctor who prescribed medicine that soon had me feeling better. I didn't feel bad my family would suffer financially that week; I was just grateful I no longer felt like I was dying.

As an adult, I know all too well that the challenges of being raised in poverty extend beyond keeping food on the table. Millions of children around the world fall into the same vicious cycle of malnourishment, tattered clothing, and lack of health care.

"Come look at what I found, Josh!" I heard one of my older brothers scream from the backyard one day.

Our yard was not your typical backyard. Only feet from the cracked concrete stairs, a circle of rocks surrounded a burned trash pile of beer cans, glass, and a variety of household goods.

"Look over here! Look what I found!" he called.

I tiptoed gingerly around the circle to where my brother was pointing. He was always getting in trouble, so I should have known better than to fall for this trick.

As soon as I noticed a snake moving its head, I jumped back, landing directly on a broken piece of a glass bottle. Adrenaline masked the pain. Looking to the ground, enough blood was gathering to form a puddle the size of my foot. Thirty seconds later, excruciating pain settled in.

My brother picked me up and ran into the bathroom, where we were joined by Robert and Dad. We placed my foot under the water faucet and watched the blood and water join in a maroon stream flowing into the drain. I remember almost fainting when my brother said, "I can see the bone." Another trip to the hospital and shots to prevent infection resulted in a loss of money for my family.

Weeks later, the stitches and wound were healing up great. Standing in line waiting to leave the classroom, a classmate started jumping up and down. He jumped into another student, tripped, and found his balance on top of my shoe. The pressure of his foot immediately stretched my stitches and reopened my wound. Blood made its way through my sock and shoe, and I headed back to the hospital, incurring more financial hardship for my family.

As intense as they were, my personal stories of hardship simply could not compare to the inspiring stories of my students. Besides Anna, another one of my students was diagnosed with multiple brain tumors requiring immediate and high-risk surgery. Even though she was faced with the challenges of having visible scars on her head and the chance the tumors would return, her joyful laughter never wavered.

I lived by, and tried to emulate, two golden principles. The first, as Grandpa always said, was "No matter how bad you have it, somebody has it worse than you." Understanding this helped bring peace and compassion to everyday life. Bad things did happen to good people, but something way worse was happening to someone else. I did my best to count my blessings, move on strong, and model this habit for my students.

The second principle was to practice empathy by thinking about my own hardships. I thought of the most painful feelings of my lifetime and applied them to the situations my students were in. Although I could truly never feel what they were feeling, I could use my personal experiences to better relate to them.

Looking back, I can't say I'm thankful I grew up in poverty, but I'm grateful I could use my past to teach life lessons. I'm also grateful for the opportunity to encourage my students to push past their pain and be the best they could be in spite of the poverty they found themselves in.

CHAPTER 9:

THE LANGUAGE OF MONEY

If you are born poor, it is not your mistake,
but if you die poor it is your mistake.

Bill Gates

Knowledge is power. The more children know about the situation they're in, the better chance they have of getting out of it.

I didn't want to simply ignore the fact that my students faced poverty every day. Rather, I wanted them to understand their environment. I wanted them to begin to understand what poverty was and how to get out of it. Take it from someone who has lived through poverty—sympathy doesn't go as far as action.

One common reason people don't leave their socio-economic class is the fear of change. Those who are raised in a lower income culture often find it difficult to adjust to a middle or upper class lifestyle. Typically, they're pressured by family members who say they're being a traitor, a sellout, or are trying to act like someone or something they're not.

In the classroom, my job was to guide my students to find solutions to the problems they faced, both in and out of the classroom. I asked questions like, "Why do you think people are poor?" and "Can they do anything about it?" I asked, "Whose fault is it?" and "Would it be scary to leave the people you've been with all your life and spend time with new people?"

The most important question I asked was, "Would you want your children to live the life you live, or do you think you can provide them with a better life?" This question was the deciding factor for several students who were ready to become the man or woman of the future who broke the chain of mediocrity in their families.

I told my students about a man who loved his family so deeply that he worked tirelessly to provide the life he believed they deserved. An electrician, he installed and repaired lighting in homes and businesses. Day after day, weekend after weekend, he responded to calls and got the job done. His knowledge of electricity was vast and he often mentored younger employees, giving them tips and tricks to the most efficient installations and repairs.

There was only one problem. This man worked for $10.00 an hour. His experience in the field gave him more knowledge than newer employees, and his skills always ensured he had a job, but he made $10.00 an hour while his co-workers with college degrees made $40.00 an hour.

The lesson was, you could be the hardest working, most honorable, and kindest person in the world. You could work thousands of hours and have employers clamoring to hire you, but this didn't mean you got paid fairly or what you were worth.

After learning about wiring and circuits in science, my students began to understand the complexity of what it would take to make the electricity work in our school. We then considered the question, "Would you rather work for $10.00 installing electricity your whole life or would you rather make $100,000.00 a year managing electricians who install the lighting?"

The answer was obvious. I needed to teach my students to work smarter and not just harder. Imagine what would happen if they worked smarter and harder at the same time!

Moving from one socioeconomic class to another brings up issues that are tough to understand, especially for children. "Is it improper to speak the way my family speaks?" a child once asked me. "My friend told me I talk 'white,'" another student commented.

How do we approach these important topics that often divide classes, races, and cultures? How do we approach these questions that are so sensitive that most teachers avoid talking about them, some out of fear of losing their jobs?

I did it by teaching a lesson I called the Language of Money, also known as Talking Green.

The Language of Money

With every student staring in awe, I threw the first $100.00 bill on the desk and said in a rough, exaggerated voice, "One hunid [hundred]."

Every student decided I'd lost my mind as I threw the next bill down, saying "Two hunid."

I continued until $3,000.00 lay spread across the desk.

"Can I ask you a question, class?" I had the attention of every child in the room so I spoke in a whisper. Playing their suspense as gingerly as I'd play the violin, I continued, "Is it okay to talk like this? To act how I just did?"

The students looked at one another. With smirks on their faces, they burst into laughter, shaking their heads no.

"Today we're going to learn about the language of money!" I said, reverting to my normal voice. "It's not about talking white, black, brown, or yellow. It's about talking green, about speaking the language of money."

My students looked puzzled.

I continued, "What if I told you that in 30 minutes, in just one interview in front of a small group of people, you could make $50,000.00?"

To looks of rapture, I explained, "You just have to speak the language of money. This is what I did." I then asked, "How do you think I spoke during my interview to get this job? Do you think I spoke as I did earlier when I was throwing the money down on the table?"

Once again I received a unanimous no.

"It's okay to talk silly to our friends," I said. "At times we even communicate differently with our own families. Sometimes we speak so strongly in the accents and culture of our families that the way we talk has nicknames. This is okay. On the other hand, it's not always proper to speak to our elders, our teachers, or people we hope will hire us in this manner. They deserve to be spoken to with respect, in the language of money."

I paused to let this information sink in.

"When you graduate from high school and college and are being interviewed for a job, you will speak the language of money," I told them. "You will talk green. You will speak how we teach you to write on paper, pronouncing your words and sitting confidently with great posture."

I jogged over to my rolling classroom chair and moved it to the center of the classroom. Putting the chair as low as the air pump would allow me, I slouched down with my arms crossed. Putting a bored expression on my face, I said, "What's up" in my deepest voice.

Laughter filled the classroom, so I used my index finger to symbolize the level at which their voice levels needed to be.

"Do I look friendly?" I asked. "Do I look like someone who is hard working and happy to be doing his job? Would you hire me?"

After another round of "No's," they began to understand that the language of money was both verbal and nonverbal.

"Now, do we have anyone who thinks they know how to sit according to the language of money? Just show me," I encouraged. "You don't need to speak to do this."

I called out the perfect examples, the students sitting up straight with smiles on their faces and complete body control.

I elaborated, "Sitting up straight shows you mean business. A smile on your face means you're happy and excited to be in the interview. Sitting still displays your discipline."

As the year progressed, we practiced each time a visitor entered the classroom. As an attention getter, I would occasionally say, "Speak the language of money." Students would immediately sit up with respectful proper postures while continuing with their work. If called upon, they spoke green, the appropriate language of respect.

For the entirety of their educations and beyond, students need to be socially aware, especially in situations such as interviews or meetings, but first they need to be taught what this means. It seems like common sense to those of us who already speak the language of money, but to many lower income students, it's a mystery. We cannot assume children are equipped with this learned skill. In the real world, we commonly take on different identities depending on the situation. Talking to a best friend is different from sitting in an interview that will determine whether or not you sign a $50,000.00 contract.

More than just teaching the curriculum, teachers must prepare today's children to enter tomorrow's world knowing what it takes to be successful.

Do your students know the language of money? Can they talk green?

Poverty is an inevitable challenge. Our job is not just to give handouts and make those in poverty feel better for a couple of days but to empower those in poverty to understand why they live this way and what it will take to create a better future for themselves and their families.

Do not just give handouts. Give people a hand up.

CHAPTER 10:

FALSE PERCEPTIONS OF SUCCESS

Dreams are merely thoughts; the doing is more powerful than the dreaming.

The doing is what changes the world and impacts people in unforeseen ways.

Mark Cuban

I was raised by my grandparents until the age of nine. After that, I moved to San Antonio with my aunts for eight years. Then I had the opportunity to move to Austin with a host family to finish high school.

I experienced every level of social class during my youth. Poverty was a reality while living with my grandparents. Middle class felt "rich" when I moved in with my aunts. Austin and private school exposed me to the wealthy class. These experiences taught me that wealth is not a given; it is earned. Some just have to work a little harder than others.

One day a student named Makayla inspired me to think more deeply about what makes a person successful when she pulled $10.00 out her pocket with a smirk on her face larger than the Grinch's.

"Are you going to share that with me?" I asked in a joking manner, raising my eyebrows and awaiting her reply.

"No way, Mr. Duncan; you're the rich one!"

"I'm not rich," I responded. I gave her a fake pout. "What should I do to get rich?"

"Ask the principal for more money because he's rich!"

I smiled. The highly entertaining conversation had gone further than I'd anticipated. "He makes great money, but he's actually not rich either," I told her.

Makayla stood with one hand on her hip, her opposite arm creating an acute angle on the side of her face, deep in contemplation.

"But now I'm confused," I continued. "If none of us are rich, then who is?"

Her response intrigued me.

"Well, you can be a basketball player or a football player or a baseball player. You can be a singer or an actor. You can be on TV and be rich."

Her ear to ear smile was back, and I chuckled to myself. For the moment, believe it or not, I had nothing to say except, "I'll think about that."

As Makayla continued in line and I walked away, her comment inspired me. Did today's children think you had to be an elite athlete or famous actor or actress to be successful and acquire great wealth?

I thought about the image of success held by my friends and peers.

I thought about my own image of the world and about all the famous musicians on my devices, TV screen, and city billboards. Was the American Dream really made up of the most beautiful and elegant men and women selling us dreams in million-dollar commercials?

If these were the people I watched, read about, listened to, and admired, if these were the people who were successful, did I have to be like them to be a true success?

I sat quietly at lunch, thinking. After school, I ran my routine two miles and got in a quick twenty-minute workout at the gym as this conversation continued cycling through my brain.

If I wasn't one of those people on television, if I wasn't an outspoken employee, if I wasn't a great public speaker, if I didn't own the nicest car and house, if I wasn't wearing the most recent trends on my back, then was I unsuccessful?

Just then, that same familiar smirk of Makayla's found its way onto my face.

I understood the world well enough to know that you didn't have to be any of these things to be successful. But I also knew that many people have an unfortunate delusion of success that is simply false. You do not have to be a professional athlete or famous musician to be successful.

Musician and actor Tyrese Gibson is known for his roles in *Transformers* and *Fast and the Furious*. I read something he once said regarding what we see when we watch the movie *Transformers*. He explained that about four or five actors or actresses are consistently on the screen but thousands of people are involved behind the scenes. The best part, he said, is that the people making the most money aren't the people on the screen. The people making the most money aren't famous, nor do they speak in front of hundreds or even thousands of people. Who are these people? The directors and producers. The companies hired to build the robots. The graphics team. There are so many more successful people than those we see as we nervously crunch our buttery popcorn during these great action movies.

I thought about one of my best friends from college. He wasn't famous, but he was one of the most successful people I knew. His journey took him from Venezuela to the United States on a school visa and scholarship for engineering. He graduated in four years, started making more than $200,000.00 a year, and has a smile on his face every time I see him. He's a walking success, but I haven't once seen him on television or listened to him through my radio speakers. I'm not even sure he's spoken in front of an audience larger than his college classroom.

Two of my best friends are in medical school. They aren't famous. They've never been on live television or spoken in front of a crowded room. Yet by the time they're 31, they'll be making an estimated $225,000.00 a year each. They are walking successes.

Some of the greatest lessons I've ever learned came from a teacher I had along the way. His advice changed my life, but he sure isn't famous.

One of my friends grew up underprivileged but consistently did his best in school and earned a scholarship to a private preparatory high school. He took advantage of his incredible mind and created an entertaining blog. After he finished law school, he started a company while teaching technology and math in China. He's hugely successful, but I'm positive he's never been on television.

We spend a lot of time and energy being entertained by those who are famous. We observe this lifestyle enjoyed by about 300 of the 7.5 billion on Earth and believe this is what life is all about. These people are only .000000042% of the people on the planet!

Mark Cuban of the Dallas Mavericks and the television show Shark Tank said, "Growing up, we are repeatedly told to dream big, to never stop dreaming, and to believe in our dreams. However, we are not told enough that dreams are accomplished by taking action...Dream of being a physical therapist; apply to physical therapy school and go from there. Dream of being a politician; get involved in local campaigns and work your way up. Dream of being a writer; apply to Elite Daily and start writing. We have more control over the 'doing' than we give ourselves credit for. If you spend all of your time dreaming, you will never grant yourself the opportunity to see what you are truly capable of accomplishing."

We need to encourage our students to dream and to dream realistically. It's okay for them to pretend they're singing on television or to imagine they're playing professional sports in front of the world. It's okay to compliment them and support their dreams. But also recognize that you can prevent them from thinking this is their only option. Show them that they don't have to be famous to live successful and fulfilling lives. It's up to parents and teachers to instill mature thinking into the minds of the young.

CHAPTER 11:

I CAN ALWAYS DO BETTER

Kindness in words creates confidence.

Kindness in thinking creates profoundness.

Kindness in giving creates love.

Lao Tzu

One day, the harsh reality of the world we live in hit me like a truck.

What seemed like a normal school day ended as usual with the school bell ringing. Most students were already on the bus and teachers were heading back to their classrooms to prepare for the next day when I noticed the police officers standing at the entryway of our school.

I looked closer and saw a Ford Expedition out front. In it were the parents of a little girl.

Another vehicle was parked out front, a government vehicle. In front of it, a little girl stood crying. A man in a suit held her by the hand. She was no more than five years old.

I watched the parents from the SUV enter the school, their voices raised as they pleaded for their daughter, but there was nothing the school could do; the court had ordered the girl to be removed from home.

I watched tears fill the little girl's eyes and stream down her cheeks. Every person who saw her must have wanted to pick her up and hug her, reassure her that everything was going to be okay, but we couldn't. The truth was, everything was not okay.

She was placed in the front seat of the blue government car. No child seat was provided. Child Protective Services was taking her away without providing a child seat? In the chaos of parents screaming, staff watching, and administration trying to handle the situation, it must have been forgotten.

Walking daily through a school filled with thousands of students offers a comfortable routine. Morning handshakes and smiles are friendly reminders that much is good in our school community. Some students smile, saying, "Hi, Mr. Duncan" and "Good morning, sir!" and "Nice shoes!" Other mornings, children are crying and I'm the one—maybe you're the one—who stops to talk.

This is why we do our jobs. This is what we love.

Seeing this little girl made me think that perhaps I can do a little better in my classroom. It made me think less about test scores and more about how to equip children with the tools to succeed in real life. It made me realize that faculty meetings and professional development are just a smaller piece of the bigger picture. It made me realize I must work harder.

I must work harder to make sure I smile at every student. I must work harder to help the student who doesn't understand how to carry numbers. I must stop what I'm doing and lend a helping hand to the crying child who is staring at the ground. Busy or not, I must work harder to never be too busy.

This child I once considered just one of thousands is now the child with a mountain to climb. She is now the child moving into the foster care system. She is now the child giving me a new perspective—the perspective that I can always do better.

One second she was smiling in class, learning to read, and the next minute she was being taken away from everything she had ever known. If we can't be compassionate, what on Earth are we here for?

Fellow teachers, past, present, and future, make the most of your influence, and do not let anyone tell you your job is not important.

CHAPTER 12:

JOE AND THE TRUE TEST OF A CHAMPION

Who is Achilles without his tendon?
Who is Samson without Delilah?

Who is Oedipus without his clubfoot?...The true hero is flawed.

The true test of a champion is not whether he can triumph,
but whether he can overcome obstacles—preferably of his own
making—in order to triumph.

Garth Stein

One year, the most popular activity among the boys was soccer. It was so popular that a teacher had to act as referee. Otherwise, the large group of 30 children would wreak havoc on one another. Imagine a pinball machine with each student's two feet as the triggers. With 60 triggers, each game was exciting and then some.

At recess one afternoon, the black and white ball rolled toward the far goal with Joe and José in close pursuit. Both of their heads were down as they looked at the ball, and naturally they collided and fell to the ground. A simple accident, you might think, but not to Joe.

This fierce athlete jumped to his feet, puffed out his chest, and assumed a stance similar to that of a king cobra threatening its enemy. Within seconds, he'd pushed José back to the ground and jumped on top of him, and the two began rolling around, battling for control.

Mr. Olavarri ran to the boys faster than his aching knee would have liked and separated them. "Off this soccer field now," he sternly ordered.

Joe screamed back with the entire fourth grade watching, "F★★★ you!"

The soccer ball was taken up and all play stopped. Joe refused to walk to the principal's office until he was hand in hand with the head of the school. This was just the beginning of his challenging year filled with battles, wins, and losses. Joe would take two steps forward and three steps back. He'd experience a day of perfection followed by a full-out meltdown.

It's only fair to provide some perspective. Our public school with high poverty rates and low incomes lacked an assistant principal, the nurse and counselor only made it out two or three days a week, and we went through three principals in one year. Turns out, Joe had more than his fair share of challenges at school and home.

First Impressions

Joe was amazing in many ways. The first day he walked through the door and into my classroom, his afro was puffed out with more style than Dr. Julius Erving himself. He was shorter than his classmates, but his hair made up for it.

The other students looked up to him. "Come on, come with me, I'll help you solve this problem," he would say. Given such confidence, no one could help but follow. With his classmates, his intelligence and social awareness were genuine and on cue. When speaking to adults, he knew just what to say. "Did you see that dunk last night Mr. 'DUNK-an?'" he'd ask me. "It was some guy on a red and white team."

Of course he was talking about the great Blake Griffin who, at the time, played for the Los Angeles Clippers. The night before, Griffin had thrown down a thunderous dunk over his opponent Kendrick Perkins. I commented, "That was pretty incredible, huh? Maybe I'll have to do that to you at recess!"

Never once did I pass up the opportunity to let Joe know he was a leader. It was imperative that he understand his peers followed in his footsteps. Like angry John, it was vital that he learn how to use his gift.

Attaining Perspective

Imagine you're sitting in a dark and peaceful room, free from all troubles. Take a few deep breaths, inhale, exhale, feel happiness. Inhale, exhale, and this time focus on the loved ones in your life. With your final breath, complete nirvana is approaching, and you vividly imagine a bright and fulfilling future. All is well until...

A switch flips. Imagine raw emotion boiling from a place deep inside, pulling you away from happiness. Imagine a raw living energy squeezing the purity out of you, pouring negative feelings into your heart, body, and soul.

You panic. The switch has been turned on! Bright agonizing light fills the room, fills you. You must react or it will kill you! It's a fight for your life, and if you don't defend yourself, it's over. You want to scream, pull your hair out, do anything to make it end.

Welcome to the mind of Joe.

Things might be going fine and then, in a snap of a finger, in the flip of a switch, all hell breaks loose. You wouldn't think a child could live through such fluctuations of emotion, such deep tormenting feelings.

Why did this happen? Why did Joe experience such extremes? Why was he able to play happily with a friend on Monday and the next day scream at him to "Shut up!" and "Stay away from me or you're gonna get hit!"?

My number one priority was to plant positive seeds in the mind of this struggling child, to create a vision for a different way of life, and, little by little, teach him how this path was much better than the previous path with rewards that were incomparable.

After just the first week of school, I knew that working with Joe would be a great and demanding challenge. I decided I would not be conquered by fear, nor would I become angry at a child who was manipulative, hurtful, and a bully. He was going through something so painful and challenging that it was difficult for others to fully understand. It was my job to help him learn how to successfully control himself and win the battle, so I wrote out a few goals to help me keep my head in the game so I wouldn't lose focus on the days Joe pushed me to the edge.

First, I reminded myself to be appreciative. I had a job. I could pay my rent. I had an awesome new car. I could afford to eat out, travel, and visit friends and family. I had clean drinking water and a decent place to live. Too often, I looked forward to the weekend and couldn't wait until the day was over. Instead, I needed to count my blessings.

Next, I reminded myself to be understanding and patient. I was working with nine- and 10-year-olds. I couldn't get frustrated at what they didn't know, forgot, or struggled to learn. My job was to help them be better than they were before, and that was it. I would not get frustrated and have unrealistic expectations. Needless to say, I practiced understanding and patience continuously, every day.

My next goal was to stay organized. Every once in a while, I would organize everything that needed to be filed away. The less clutter, the more space to think.

Finally, I wanted to be a role model. My goal was to create great leaders who could live happily. There was too much hatred and negativity in the world, too many people who didn't have the confidence to say no to what they knew was wrong. I needed to help my students believe in themselves, to know their decisions would have good and bad consequences, and to have the intelligence and self-control to make good choices.

Getting Creative

"Six foot, seven foot, eight foot, nine!" Joe shouted while the class was in route to physical education, disrupting every classroom on both sides of the hallway.

I walked right next to him, bent down so he could hear me, and whispered, "Joe, please do not raise your voice in the hallway, especially when it's a song that's inappropriate for school. Everyone else knows they have to follow hallway expectations, and you're no different."

The average student would have immediately apologized, become part of the perfect line, and silently moved down the hall, but not Joe.

Instead, he burst out with "Lil' Wayne is the man!" and proceeded with a chuckle.

When we arrived at P.E., I sent the other students on and pulled Joe to the side. "I politely asked you to stop speaking in the hallway and told you my expectations. Your recess time will be reduced and your discipline folder will be written in. There is a time to speak, and the hallway is not one of them."

After school, I told Joe I'm a fan of a rapper named Lupe Fiasco. Fiasco has a song about skateboarding that students like, he rarely uses foul language, and his lyrics contain quality meanings such as "I believe in the world" or "the ink of a scholar is worth a thousand times the blood of a martyr." While this artist isn't perfect, if Joe was going to listen to rap, I'd rather have him listening to positive and thought-provoking messages than the song he'd been singing in the hallway.

Suddenly, I had an idea. If Joe enjoyed rap music, then he probably enjoyed the play on words that was common in rap songs. In the song he'd been singing, one of the lyrics went, "real g's move in silence like lasagna."

The next day, when Joe finished his math work early, I told him I had a riddle for him to figure out. He was game, so I wrote in his spiral, "G's are silent like lasagna" and explained, "I'm going to give you three minutes to discover the meaning behind this phrase. If you succeed, you get to eat lunch with me and I'll pay for it."

He was thrilled.

"Go," I said and started the stopwatch.

Joe's mind was churning. He was intent on his paper. A minute passed, and his eyes hadn't moved from the phrase; the incentive was too great not to give it his full effort. "Lasagna, lasagna, lasagna," he kept repeating.

"Thirty seconds left! Focus on how the word is spelled," I said. "Ten, nine, eight…three, two, one. Time's up."

Joe dropped his pencil in frustration. "Okay, what is it?" he asked.

"Sound out lasagna for me, letter by letter, loud enough for me to hear you."

"La-a-s-a-n." He stopped. "There isn't a 'g' in lasagna!"

"Oh, but there is," I responded. "I wrote it right there in your spiral. When you say 'lasagna,' you can't hear the 'g'; it's silent."

His face cleared and he smiled. He understood. "Come on, Mr. Duncan, give me another chance."

The challenge was a success. I'd been able to create a learning opportunity using culture and interest for a child who had experienced challenges in his life most nine-year-olds couldn't imagine. Any opportunity to challenge him with something he could relate to or thought was "cool" was helpful.

The rap lyric was also an opportunity to teach him that what he heard in lyrics or saw in music videos wasn't real, a common misconception among lower income students. I explained that musicians are surrounded by cameras and directed how to act.

"It's all like a movie, Joe," I told him. "The songs and lyrics are a story; it's usually not real life. If the things they spoke about in their lyrics were true, they would be in a bad place such as prison."

Joe had a lot to learn, and he was just starting to trust me as a successful and happy adult who could help guide him.

That fall, before the mandated parent/teacher night, I scheduled a meeting with Joe's mom to talk about the numerous situations Joe had been involved in that had already required a phone call home. I didn't want to take any chances that she might not attend.

The evening arrived, we introduced ourselves, and Jennifer, Joe's mom, immediately began the conversation.

"Thank you so much for all you do for my son! I can't tell you how happy I am when I don't receive a call from school saying Joe has gotten in trouble or that I need to come pick him up. It's tough with work and all."

Slowly but surely, I'd learned that you're never going to get through to someone if you focus on the negatives, so I confidently responded, "Joe is definitely a character. He brings so much to the table! The other students look up to him, and he is socially ahead of the game."

An ear-to-ear smile appeared on her face. Seeing her joy upon hearing great things about her child was indescribable. It was almost as if she were hearing compliments about herself. It was also apparent that Jennifer had come in expecting a grilling, the kind she was used to when it came to her son. Angry staff members typically blamed her and began venting about her son without giving her suggestions on how to resolve the challenges.

My approach was different. From the start of the meeting, she knew I was on her side and that I wanted to work together to turn Joe's life around. I told her, "We do have some issues to tackle. Although Joe is incredibly smart, he sometimes lacks the work ethic to complete his assignments. He often gets into conflicts with other students, and he often instigates them himself. Do you have any ideas or suggestions on where to begin changing his attitude?"

To my surprise, the same look I saw in Joe' eyes when he was getting close to losing control appeared on Jennifer's face. Fear began to grow in my stomach in the form of butterflies. I was all ears, waiting for her to say something powerful, and she did.

"Joe comes home and tells me he is getting bullied by other students. He is defending himself! Last year two students from this school beat him up!"

This was news to me, so I nodded and responded with a simple "Wow."

She continued, "I know how this feels. His father used to abuse me, hit me, yell at me, and Joe unfortunately had to see this." Tears began pouring from her eyes and she said, "I'm not going to put up with anyone taking advantage of me, and Joe is the same way."

Things were starting to make sense.

She continued, "I stood up for myself, and he is going to do the same. But he acts a lot like his father. The cursing, the fighting, are all just like his dad. I talked to him and told him he needs to clean up his act, but I can't control what Joe sees when he visits his father."

It would take weeks for me to fully digest everything Joe's mom shared that evening, but I knew we had to take a positive approach and help Joe one step at a time. I told her, "Thank you for sharing all this. You didn't have to, but you chose to because it's in Joe's best interests that we understand him so we can pursue a better and successful future for him."

I told her I wanted to talk to Joe about his actions and create some goals. I would help him brainstorm what he thought was great in his life. When he began to feel down or angry, he could look at his blessings, only a paper's reach away.

Jennifer agreed to this plan, gave me multiple phone numbers, and insisted the staff at school keep her updated as much as possible. She wasn't perfect, but her intentions were good.

Growing Pains

The following day, Joe stayed after school. We sat down together and I told him, "Your mom and I spoke yesterday, and both of us want what's best for you—we want you to be successful."

Joe and I talked about what success means and came to the conclusion that success is how happy a person is.

I then asked him, "What seems to be the problem for you when it comes to being happy?"

I was surprised when he said, "I just want the other fourth graders to like me, Mr. Duncan."

His words were consistently hurtful to other students, he made fun of girls, and he told others to stay away from him. How could he possibly care what other students thought of him?

Then I realized what the problem was. Joe lacked confidence. That's why he acted out.

Too many times in the middle of a lecture, Joe would think a student across the room was looking at him with malicious intent. He would then abruptly shout, "What are you looking at?"

His assumptions were illogical. The last time this had happened in class, I'd explained, "If you see Kobe Bryant walking down the street, are you going to look at him? Ladies, if you see Beyonce strutting, waving her long hair side to side, are you going to stop and stare?"

Giggles had filled the room as the students imagined themselves in the presence of someone famous.

A boy had raised his hand and said, "Yea, I'm going to stare; Kobe Bryant is the best player ever."

"Exactly," I'd responded while a girl in the back of the classroom raised her hand and moved it back and forth, imitating the dance to Beyonce's single "All the Single Ladies."

"Do you think either one of these people gets mad when others look at them?" I'd asked rhetorically. "Absolutely not! They know they're not being looked at because something is wrong. They're being looked at because they're great. They're being looked at because people like something about them. I challenge you to take that perspective."

I'd gazed directly at Joe. "When someone is looking at you, don't immediately think they don't like you. Start believing they see something special in you. Maybe they think you're cool or they like something you're wearing. Be confident!"

I decided to focus on having Joe evaluate the consequences of reacting to students he thought were staring at him from across the room. I didn't focus on whether he was right or wrong but rather on whether it was worth losing happiness and peace of mind for something minuscule and irrelevant to the path of success he wanted to pave.

I never wanted to lecture my students or focus on their problems. Instead, I wanted to focus on a plan that would help them take responsibility and ownership for their actions and figure out how to fix them. If Joe wasn't going to follow through on the ideas he came up with, he wouldn't be failing me; he'd simply be failing himself. It was his choice whether his classmates accepted him or not.

I told Joe we were going to create something called *Joe's Reminders of Success*, and he was excited. First, I asked him to list reasons why his classmates might not like him, and it was a revelation for Joe to realize there were lots of reasons! Next, we created solutions through actions that would help him avoid feeling unaccepted.

The most important element of *Joe's Reminders of Success* was the section about counting blessings. We titled this section "Confident Joe."

The first three blessings Joe listed were all family related. Little things like this helped remind me that people are kind at heart, especially when they're children. For a child his age not to mention money, toys, or friends said a lot about him. Joe loved his mom and sister with all his heart although he didn't always show this the best way. We talked about how his actions affected his mom when she had to leave work and worry about how her son was behaving in school. He showed maturity in his thinking, and with a small amount of guidance, he named several positive aspects of his life.

With perfect timing, our new principal walked past the room. It would be great for her to see what Joe was working on, so I called out, "Ms. Perez, Joe has been working on some goals for the classroom this year. Want to come check it out?"

She responded, "Oh, ya, tell me about it, Joe."

He spoke confidently. "I'm going to start doing a better job in school. I want my mom to be happy and I want all my friends to like me."

She responded, "That's great, Joe. I'm glad you're taking steps to improve yourself. I knew you had it in you."

We completed *Joe's Reminders of Success* and left extra room on the last page for him to fill in more things he was thankful for at a later date.

I printed three copies. Joe was to keep his with him at all times and resort to it anytime something troubled him at school. He had permission to stop anything he was doing if he needed to grab his copy and begin reading what was important to him. Hopefully, this reminder of how successful he wanted to be and how many blessings he had would ease the pressure when negative feelings suddenly arose.

The second copy was for his mom. She could keep it at home or work and use it as necessary when she spoke to Joe.

The third copy would stay with me at my desk. I would use it as a reminder when I noticed something was agitating Joe. I would kindly point to the list and redirect him as necessary.

Joe's phone lit up with the title "Mom" displayed in the middle of the screen. He answered and told his mom, "I'm on my way out now."

Joe and I walked together to the edge of the street where his mom was waiting in the driver's seat of her small compact car. As Joe walked around to the passenger seat, Jennifer and I started to converse.

"How was Joe today?" she asked.

"He was awesome. We just finished up working on something special. I kept a copy, Joe has one of his own, and here is yours."

I handed the paper to her and explained, "These two pages are all Joe's thoughts and ideas; I can't take too much credit."

She skimmed through the packet and reached the second page where Joe had listed his blessings. A tear fell from her eye as she reached over and hugged him. She turned to me and said, "Thank you so much for your time, Mr. Duncan. This is going to make a big difference."

As they drove off, I thought to myself, "Step by step and day by day." I understood that this was a big step. I also understood there was no way to magically solve all Joe's troubles at once. He was an amazing and complex person whose maturity would take time. Nonetheless, he was on his way. The following is *Joe's Reminders of Success*.

<u>Success</u> = How Happy You Are
What is the problem?

1. Left out when others get to play.

2. Laughing at or with other students who are making distracting noises.

3. Calling others crybaby or tattletale.

4. Making fun of others because they are talking about me or because I can make others laugh by making fun of others.

How will we fix this?

1. Bad behavior makes me sit out. If I practice strategies to success, I'll never have to sit out again!

2. Laughing is a good thing but is it worth it? Is it worth having to sit out because of another person's actions?

They will sit out from recess but I won't have to. I am awesome at soccer and I want to play!

3. Others will tell Mr. Duncan what I did and I will agree with them when I did something wrong. I will get mad because I don't want to sit out of recess or get in trouble at home. I can fix this by changing my actions and not doing something that would make them tell Mr. Duncan on me. If they do something bad, I will tell Mr. Duncan.

4. When others talk about me, it makes me feel sad. When I talk about them, it makes them feel sad. I can fix this by <u>being a leader</u> and ignoring them. <u>I am awesome, athletic, smart, funny, musically inclined, and have a friendly personality.</u>

Confident Joe

I have so many awesome things in my life that I should not be worried about the few small things that happen. <u>I will be a leader and ignore the small things!</u> "Count your blessings and do not dwell in the disasters."

1. I like living with my mom and sister!

2. I get to see my dad on the weekends!

3. I have family. Some people are adopted or don't even have a family.

4. I like sports and can play and watch them on T.V.

5. Other friends, ones who trust me and know I will always be there for them, play sports with me so I can get better like Mr. Duncan balling on the soccer field.

6. I'm healthy, I can walk, I'm not in a hospital, and I don't have asthma so I can run!

7. I love music and can always listen to it. I understand success is what I can do to be happy and not what I hear in songs. Some music is like a movie.

8. I have goooooood food! Some people are fighting for life and dying from hunger.

9. ?

10. ?

Joe could only come up with eight things for his "Awesome" list, but he left room at the bottom to add more.

Balancing Act

More than 50 students came in and out of my room a thousand times each year. Some were teacher's pets and some were introverts. Some couldn't sit still or follow normal procedures yet still managed to pull straight A's. Some were poor and disadvantaged yet maintained a great work ethic. Some were troubled, consistently disrespectful, refused to work, and spoke negatively to peers and elders.

Personally, my greatest challenge as a teacher and leader was managing so many different personalities all at once. I only had two hands, one mind, one soul, and a limited amount of energy. How could I create as much greatness as possible while rescuing troubled students from their slow descent to failure? My favorite reminder to greatness, something called the 5 P's, or Proper Preparation Prevents Poor Performance, only went so far.

A part of me said to forget these angry children. I asked myself, "Do people ever really change? Am I wasting my energy trying to help them succeed?" Let me remind you, these were doubts and not reality.

On the other end of the spectrum were the students who followed all the rules. They were always willing to give a helping hand and all they had on each and every assignment. Shouldn't these students get all the attention? Shouldn't all my energy go towards the kids who were ready to learn?

I was spending more and more time on children who interrupted classroom activities, distracted students and staff, and refused to complete classroom assignments. The respectful and prepared scholars sitting quietly waiting for my instructions were being held back because of the behavior of classmates and the lack of staff to handle behavior problems.

The advice I gave mature students was, "Compare the classroom to real life. There are distractions in both places along with good and bad people. As we speak, you are already choosing who you're going to be. Like me, you're already on the journey to greatness. Your work ethic will only grow with time, school will come easier, and when you're an adult, you will become a success. You can do anything you want. Just know that it's up to you and that it starts right now. Be great!"

I then corrected myself. "No," I said. "Stay great!"

CHAPTER 13:

THE POWER OF WORDS

*It is the supreme art of the teacher to awaken joy
in creative expression and knowledge.*

Albert Einstein

In 2011, more than 3,100 prisoners in the city of Dallas came from 10 area zip codes. According to studies by the Texas Education Agency, these 10 areas also had 3,000 students in the 2011 graduating class, and only 26 of them were "college ready."

If you lived in one of the many neighborhoods in these 10 zip codes, you were almost guaranteed a life of struggle, prison, lack of encouragement and expectation, malnourishment, and a hole that grew deeper every day of your life. The *Dallas Morning News* called this situation the "Cradle to Prison Pipeline."

The school I taught in was in one of these zip codes. All my students lived here. Joe lived here. Could Joe be one of the 26?

Could he defy the odds? Could he get out? And what about everyone else?

One day, Joe had a disagreement with a classmate. Instead of focusing on the issue at hand, he turned his classmate's physical scars into a joke, calling him "Scar face" and laughing excessively. With *Joe's Reminders of Success* in my hand, I asked Joe to explain what he was feeling and thinking when he called the other student that hurtful name.

"I don't like him anyway; he was talking about my mom. I'll hit him, I swear I'll hit him, just watch."

"What's that going to do, Joe?" I asked. "Isn't our goal to make friends, not enemies? You're going to let one little thing ruin your day? The actions of one person are going to completely dictate who you become? There are seven billion people on earth. *Seven billion.* Do you realize how many that is?"

He didn't. I told him, "Imagine walking down a beautiful beach. Imagine a single grain of sand blows through the air and hits you in the eye. Are you going to let one grain of sand out of billions of grains effect how you feel about the rest of the beach? Are you going to stomp off and be mad for a minute, an hour, the rest of the day, or forever just because of one grain?"

Joe shook his head, his brown eyes attentive.

"Stop letting what someone else says or does change who you are. For the rest of your life, you're going to run into people you don't get along with. If you let them get to you, you'll never be able to reach your goals."

I gave him another analogy. "Every day, people drive to work or school. Say a car accidentally cuts you off. Are you going to start screaming and cursing? You can't control the other driver's mistakes or aggressive driving. Should you allow one bad driver to ruin your day? We only have control over ourselves. In the words of actor and rapper Will Smith, 'Stop letting people who do so little for you control so much of your mind, feelings, and emotions.'"

I let Joe know I would have to call his mom and that he would have to talk with the counselor. He would also have to apologize to the other student for his hurtful words.

Aggression among males in lower income areas has always been high. A study done by Rice University followed 13 high-income families, 10 middle-income families, 13 low-income families, and six families who were on welfare over a span of four years. One finding was that children in higher income households hear 30 million more words in the first four years of life than children living in lower income households.

Words are knowledge, and knowledge is power. Power is choice, and choice is freedom. The opportunity to hear more words, listen to more stories, and learn about other people's journeys to greatness empowers students to make good decisions in bad situations.

If someone tells me my mom is ugly, I'm not worth a penny, and I should crawl in a hole and die, it's not going to end my world. My first thought will probably be, "Wow, I wonder why this person is so angry?"

This is because I know one person's words cannot make a significant difference in the outcome of my being. I understand that they are just one person out of billions and their opinion is irrelevant to my journey through life. I also recognize that the world is full of kind people who are willing to give their energy to make me a better person. It would be completely immature of me to become consumed with one negative person's opinion.

Yet families with lower incomes statistically have limited vocabularies. Their kids hear fewer stories and learn about fewer journeys to greatness. The idea of planting a seed and harvesting it at a later date is unclear. Without the opportunity to see, read about, or directly know someone who is successful, it's almost impossible not to become offended at another person's hurtful words or actions.

Lack of opportunity, lack of resources, and lack of knowledge create a chain that has continued to link in lower income families for decades and even centuries without being broken. Parents and educators are key to breaking the shackles and encouraging our youth to learn about others who have found a way to rise from their difficult environments.

The moment my students walked into my room and began working on their assignments, they knew I expected their best. They had to think as hard as they could even if they were struggling. They weren't motivated by a fear of being punished but instead by the fact that I believed in them. I expected them to make smart decisions, and they knew they had someone rooting them on. Every day, I encouraged them with positive words and taught them to practice the characteristics of successful people.

During the first week of every school year, I made it a priority to give my students reasons why we studied math. Who wanted to practice something every day, put in hours of work, sweat, and tears, without knowing why? Does a star-powered NBA team behind Lebron James start a season of agonizing workouts and muscle-pounding efforts without first having a goal of winning the championship? No way.

I wanted my students to envision their destination, their goals, and see how math played a vital role in their success. Even though they were only nine and 10 years old, I believed in their ability to think at a high level. They were all intrigued by how the real world worked, and it was my job to show them they had the opportunity to succeed and, in cases like Joe's, break the chain of mediocrity in their families. I decided to teach a lesson on budgeting I called Money Talks.

Money Talks

"How much do you think I make a year?" I asked the class.

"Ten thousand dollars!" a student shouted.

Shaking my head, I said, "Raising our hands, let's take another guess."

"Twenty-five thousand dollars," Olivia guessed.

From the first two responses, it was easy to see my fourth graders didn't have a clear understanding of incomes or standards of living.

"Forty-six thousand dollars a year," I whispered, raising my eyebrows to the heavens as the words slipped off my tongue.

To them, this was a fortune. I could only imagine the enormous pile of money they were envisioning.

I explained how my taxes and health insurance were deducted from my paycheck, leaving me with about $3,000.00

every month. Then I said, "Can I ask you guys to help me do something? I need to figure out how much money I have left over at the end of the month after I pay my bills, and I need some smart mathematicians to assist me. Let's title our papers 'Budget.'"

When this was done, I asked, "What are some things I have to pay for each month?"

Having seen me driving to school in the morning with my sunroof pulled back, a student raised her hand and said, "Maybe your car?"

"Very good, Tierra. Every month I have to make a payment on my car in the amount of $417.00." I wrote down "car," put the total next to it, and asked my students to do the same.

"Now what happens if someone accidentally hits my car and I need to get it fixed?"

Almost every hand in the classroom excitedly began waving around like a newly sprung Jack-in-the-Box. I got the correct answer and replied, "Insurance, yes, very important because we know that accidents happen and we always want to be prepared for them."

Slowly but surely, we compiled an accurate list of payments most adults have each month. Besides car payment and insurance, the list included rent, cable, water, phone, gas, my gym membership, healthy food, and last but not least, my school loans.

With all the bills written down, the students added them up and came to the conclusion that $46,000.00 wasn't as much as they'd originally thought. I took the opportunity to begin teaching them about the importance of saving, budgeting, and avoiding credit card interest rates.

Subsequently, 90% of the class passed the daily assessment on why math is an imperative part of becoming a successful adult.

I had high expectations for every child, including Joe, from the first day they walked in my room. It's more helpful for children to understand how the real world operates instead of living in a fantasy land of books, test sheets, and numbers that ignore the tools that will help them succeed in life. Books, test sheets, and meaningless numbers become valuable learning tools only when students understand why they're important.

A lack of practical knowledge is detrimental to the success of lower income students. Parents don't always have the knowledge to equip their children with the tools to be successful, and to be honest, many teachers don't either. The teachers who do have the knowledge don't always have the time to teach such valuable lessons because they're too busy trying to achieve the best possible results on standardized tests.

At the same time, can teachers blame the administration when regional directors pressure principals and superintendents who are paid by how well their districts perform on national tests?

We forget that students need people who believe in them enough to encourage them to overcome their impoverished backgrounds and develop the same higher level thinking skills that privileged children more readily develop. Ever more test-taking strategies do not teach lower income students that they have a choice in who they want to be and can leave their current situations instead of just becoming another statistic.

A friend of mine once said, "If you can't see yourself in the palace, you'll never have the courage to leave the fields." He explained that I was doing more than just educating students on a given topic; I was helping them believe they deserved to be in the palace.

My goal was to begin the process of helping all the Joes in my classroom develop the belief that they could let go of their troubles and begin embracing life's gifts. Most of all, my goal was to teach them how to be confident in themselves.

Glimmers of Change

As the school year ended, glimmers of change began to show. Joe, along with several others, had begun to say "Please" and "Thank you," to raise his hand before speaking, and most importantly, to apologize for his bad behaviors. He was beginning to recognize the difference between right and wrong, the first steps toward taking responsibility for himself.

I've always said the greatest teachers teach children how to teach themselves. The greatest teachers instill in students the tools they need to chip away at the obstacles life throws their way. The greatest teachers do not just have students who pass state exams required by the education system. Their students participate in a year of confidence-building activities that encourage a strong work ethic and successful habits.

As I turned the key in the classroom lock and began pulling it out for the last time that year, I heard a familiar voice down the hall. It was Jennifer, Joe's mom.

Some of my colleagues were in the habit of scampering away before the parent of a difficult student saw them, but that wasn't my approach. Instead, I walked over to Jennifer and gave her a big hug.

"Wow, what a year it's been. I have been in contact with you more than anyone else." I said this with a non-judgmental smile, and she smiled in return before thanking me for the support I'd given Joe.

I told her, "We have grown so much this year. I've grown, you've grown, and most of all Joe has grown. He is a child learning to find his way, and it's a little harder for some than others."

I reminded her that while Joe had been in my classroom for a year, he would have some of these staff members until he moved to middle school, but then we'd all be gone. Teachers would be in and out of his life for years to come, but she would be his only constant. I encouraged her to continue to be strong, to practice his goals with him, and to never fail to remind him that she expected great things from him.

"Maintaining high yet realistic expectations is a must. It's been an amazing year," I told her. We hugged again and parted ways.

That following summer was a time of growth for me. I was relocated within the district to a different school with a higher student population and the need for a strong fourth grade teacher. My new work family was awesome, but I missed my old school.

Feeling a little nostalgic early that fall, I made a call to my co-worker Andy to check on my old team and see how things were going.

I was thrilled when he told me the students had reacted well to new school policies and were adjusting to the discipline system. Then he said, "You'll never imagine who's almost perfect this year!"

In the back of my head I was thinking, *Let it be Joe. Could it be Joe? There's no way he could be talking about Joe already.*

"It's Joe," Andy confirmed. "Something has gotten into him, and it's definitely for the better. I talked to his mom. We think it had a lot to do with the realization that summer school isn't fun when he'd rather be playing with friends."

This was music to my ears. I responded, "Either way, what an incredible change. Look how much he's overcome in just a year."

"He's not perfect, but compared to last year, he's a brand new person."

That was all I needed to hear. All the work the staff and I had put into helping Joe was paying off, and one day he would be truly grateful for it. When this moment came to pass, the energy he gave back to others would be incredible. He could change hundreds, thousands, and possibly millions of lives, and he began his personal journey to greatness with his teachers.

Always remember, in the end, your energy is not a waste of time.

CHAPTER 14:

CREATING INDEPENDENT THINKERS

*No one is born hating another person because of the color
of his skin, or his background, or his religion.*

*People must learn to hate, and if they can learn to hate,
they can be taught to love, for love comes more naturally to the
human heart than its opposite.*

Nelson Mandela

The lack of independence and self-sufficiency I saw in my students was a consistent problem at the beginning of every school year. How could I teach required lessons and stay on course with state and national standards when my students hadn't yet developed the necessary tools for problem solving?

At the beginning of each year, it required a full hour to dissect and complete a single word problem. I helped guide students using a series of questions, but I refused to give out answers. This created panic early on, but by December, most dependent students had begun to think independently.

Nonetheless, it was always a challenge convincing my administration that we were behind because I was building tools such as confidence, independence, and critical thinking that would help us have a successful second half of the year.

A mentor and school leader shared with me, "Our goal is not to give our students the exact tool each time they have a problem to solve. Our goal is to help them acquire a tool belt with numerous tools they have learned to use. When they come upon a problem that needs solving, they can choose from a variety of tools that fit the job, allowing them to complete the task independently." This reminded me of the parable, "Give a man a fish and he will eat for a day, but teach a man to fish, and he will eat for a lifetime."

One memorable way I worked to create independent thinkers challenged my students to rise above their socioeconomic status and become financially successful. This lesson encouraged them to think above and beyond their current situations and ask questions to figure out how to get where they wanted to be. I called this lesson "Because They Are Rich."

Because They Are Rich

Poverty is a vicious cycle for millions of families, and it impacts more than just one generation at a time. According to the National Center for Children in Poverty, a child's future economic position is strongly influenced by that of his or her parents. In fact, in 2009, the latest year for which comprehensive data is available, 42% of children born to parents in the bottom fifth of the economic distribution remained in the bottom as adults and another 23% rose only to the second fifth.

Meanwhile, 39% of children born to parents at the top of the income distribution remained at the top with another 23% moving to the second fifth.

In other words, children raised in poverty had an incredibly higher chance of remaining in poverty as adults than children born in average-income to wealthy households.

The famous musician Jack Johnson said, "Every hero starts from the bottom." This might be true. The problem is, many also stay at the bottom, never finding a way out of poverty.

In my four and a half years in the classroom, I taught more than 200 students who lived in poverty. What difference did I make? Let's do some basic math.

Say those two hundred students grow to become adults, marry, and have four children each. Two hundred adults, a spouse, and four children brings us to 1,200 people directly influenced. And the cycle continues. Imagine the significance a lifetime educator can have on the students and families involved!

More elegantly phrased, positively impacting a student can change generations, a benefit that continues to exponentially grow.

Here's an example of how I worked to create independent thinkers. One day, after helping my students solve three math problems in a row, I asked them to complete a problem on their own. When I walked around my classroom, I saw most of my students staring at a blank sheet of paper. I said, "I've helped you solve three problems. Now I'm asking you to complete one by yourself and I see nothing, not even an attempt? It looks as though you don't care enough to even try."

After a pause in which no one said a word, I said, "If I took this math problem to Highland Park, do you think their fifth grade students would solve it quickly and correctly?" Highland Park is an upper-class school district prominent in the Dallas area.

Seven hands immediately began waving.

"Kristen," I called.

"I think they'd solve it," she said, bending her neck and raising her shoulder so high it nearly touched her big smile.

"Mike," I called on a second student.

"They would solve it really fast," he responded so enthusiastically that his friends laughed at his goofy facial expression.

"Okay, any other thoughts?"

A steady hand calmly went up. The class athlete and "cool kid" was going to speak.

"No question in my mind. They are going to get the problem right."

Three volunteers, and all three said the "rich student" would get the problem correct.

"Why do you think rich kids can solve this problem when you won't even try? Don't get me wrong," I said. "A few of you were solving it and your hard work will pay off, but as for the rest of you, why can the Highland Park students solve this problem correctly but you can't?"

"Because they are rich," one of my students said.

"Because they are rich," I repeated with a look of confusion, tilting my head back and shooting my eyebrows straight to the ceiling.

"Okay. They're rich," I shrugged. "Why does this enable them to solve math problems that we won't even try? Does money make them smarter than us?"

A quiet student raised his hand and shared, "They have more money than us. They can afford more...you know." He pointed around to the technology in the classroom.

"Wait a second!" I said. "We have thousands of dollars' worth of technology in our classroom, including six computers. It isn't a technology problem."

Whispers spread, then Marcy stated, "People aren't smarter just because of the things they have."

"So what else could it be? What enables these students you call 'rich' to answer these math problems correctly?"

One of my brightest students raised her hand. "It's because of their parents. Their parents can help them at home. Their parents have high expectations. If they have successful parents, then they know they can be successful."

I was elated. This was exactly the answer I wanted.

"That is exactly right," I replied. "These students know what success looks like because they have parents and even grandparents who sacrificed and worked hard to put themselves and their kids in a great position. These so-called rich people are successful because of their resilient work ethic. They've gone to college. They've budgeted like we've talked about in class. They've pursued prestigious careers such as medicine, law, business, engineering, and education while showing their children they can do the exact same thing. These rich people weren't just born successful. They worked hard to get what they have!"

The students sat quietly, intrigued by the discussion but perplexed as to where it was leading.

"These rich people are *you!*" I pointed one by one at every child in my room until I'd listed every child's name. "You are rich, Yolanda. You are rich, Joe. You are rich, Will. You are rich, Kim. You are rich, Kole. You are rich, Cassie. You are rich, Paulo." A huge smile appeared on every face as my students exchanged high fives and handshakes.

I concluded, "You are rich because *you* are going to be successful adults and parents. I will teach you how to budget and save your money and even give you lessons on investing. I will teach you how to go to college and pay for it. I will help you understand what you're great at and give you a list of professions that will pay you to do what you love. I will give you the keys to become successful adults, but you will need to work hard and use them!"

Even though my colleagues and I were using every method known to mankind to increase test scores, many of our students continuously failed to try because we were ignoring the root cause of underachieving in our urban communities: our students had not learned to think independently, work hard, and believe in themselves. At their core, they had yet to build the confidence to succeed independently.

Real Questions Inspire Real Thinking

We started each morning in the classroom with a bell ringer followed by a morning meeting where we covered topics such as how to shake hands while meeting and greeting others. Sometimes these lighthearted moments inspired serious questions.

Michael raised his hand one day. "Mr. Duncan, why do white people hate black people?"

An uproar quickly filled the room.

There are thousands of potential responses to such a question based on the type of teacher you are and your knowledge of the subject. The safest route is to respond with, "Perhaps you can go speak to the counselor about your thoughts."

I didn't want to take the safe route. I found the question intriguing. A kind and well-behaved student had sincerely asked what was on his mind. Whether this was what he had learned from his parents or was an outgrowth of images he saw on television, it had planted a seed of fear in his heart. I could leave this seed alone or I could address it. As an educator, I knew that if one student had a misconception, so did others, so I chose to address it.

Calming the class, I said, "Michael has a sincere concern, and I'm glad he took the time to share it. Michael, why do you feel that white people hate black people?"

Michael responded, "I keep seeing white cops killing black people."

His classmates were silent, a look of concern on their faces. Some were afraid Michael had gone too far. Others shared Michael's fear.

I responded, "Where do you see this?"

"All over Facebook and it's always on the news," he replied.

"Has anyone else seen this?"

Numerous hands flew up and statements began flying.

"The guy in the hoody was killed!"

"The police choked that man to death."

"He was on the ground when they shot him!"

Another student raised her hand. "This is scary. Why do we have to talk about this?"

I allowed anyone who was uncomfortable to leave the room, and then William raised his hand. When I called on him, he turned to Michael and said, "What you are saying is very racist."

I nodded. "I can see how what he's saying might sound racist, but many people think white people hate black people, so it's important to talk about this. We've all seen videos of police officers who are supposed to protect our citizens actually hurting them or taking their lives." Every head nodded, so I took a deep breath and continued.

"Recently, several white police officers accused of taking the lives of black citizens have been on the news. Some of these officers are evil people who don't deserve to wear a badge, but let me ask you: do a few terrible police officers make all police officers bad? Does one bad apple ruin the entire tree? In other words, is it fair if three of you are misbehaving to make the entire class miss recess?"

Students vehemently shook their heads. They understood how unfair this was.

"We have between 750,000 and 800,000 law enforcement officers serving in the United States." I wrote the numbers on the board. We were learning about place values, and this was a perfect opportunity to emphasize math in the real world.

"No one really knows how many criminal cops there are in the country," I went on. "People are just starting to track the numbers, and police agencies themselves seldom keep this data."

I then asked the students to estimate the number of stories in the news that covered white police and black victims. Of the billions of potential topics that could be covered, I received an average guess of police brutality being covered about 50% of the time.

"These terrible situations are blinding us to the many white and black communities that support one another as fellow Americans. I'm not saying we should ignore issues that need coverage, but what about the many fine police officers we never hear a word about? How often do we see videos celebrating officers in our community? How often does the media show the African American population supporting law enforcement, grateful for the safety they provide to our communities? This support happens all over America every day."

We then discussed the rioting in Baltimore after the death of Freddie Gray. We discussed the fact that social media and the news focused on close-ups of angry citizens destroying what others had taken lifetimes to build. I asked my students, "Why didn't the news show that the majority of citizens in Baltimore safely protested and maturely handling the situation? Why did the media only cover stories of hate, fear, and violence that didn't accurately depict reality?"

My students and I discussed the power of fear. We concluded that people respond to fear quickly as well as to extreme cases of hate and violence. We discussed how, when people sense potential threats to their safety, they become consumed by news sources and social media that cover these threats.

I asked my students to consider two scenarios and how they would be treated in the news. In the first scenario, a white officer saves the life of an elderly black woman as he carries her from a burning house. In the second scenario, a white officer harms an unarmed black teen.

My students agreed that the first story would be short lived and would quickly fade. It might make the morning news and maybe go viral for a week, but then it would be forgotten.

By contrast, everyone agreed that the story in the second scenario would be the headliner in the newspaper, on TV, and all over the internet. Unlike the story of the elderly black lady being saved by a white police officer, this story of violence would survive much longer.

I explained what mass numbers of viewers and clicks sound like to news sources and social media companies—the "cha-ching" of a cash register. I explained that every news source is a business, and businesses rely on numbers. The more viewers they have, the more they can charge for commercials and sponsors. The more clicks they get, the more advertisements they can sell and place on their websites.

I told my students, "The largest television networks will begin to advertise the upcoming interviews with the family of the young African American teen harmed by police officers. Anticipation will build as people want to hear what this heartbroken mother has to say. Will she be angry? Will she be sad? Will she say something unifying? Will she say something destructive? All the while, sponsors who want to reach millions of viewers will advertise their products on these news stations."

Through our discussion, my students came to understand that the challenging topic of white police officers harming unarmed blacks must be discussed and confronted and that reform must happen, yet they also came to understand that we need to find ways to affirm the good that is happening between and among races. I told them, "Sometimes I see a Facebook picture or video of white police officers in an African American neighborhood playing basketball or football with the kids. These types of interactions are happening too, but they seldom make the news."

Finally, my students concluded that bad people aren't bad because of the color of their skin. They began to understand that every race has bad people but that this doesn't make the entire race bad.

It was important for our class to have this conversation. Otherwise, many of my students might have grown into adults who feared others because of their race and color. Because of this discussion and others like it, I hoped my students would develop the habit of looking deeper into the issues and forming educated positions and opinions.

Knowledge is power. Young people need to know what is going on in the world around them and how to think critically about it.

Challenge Them to Think

Perhaps society is to blame for the attitude of "I want it now and I want it quick!" The fact is, our consumer-based society demands immediate satisfaction.

Every fast food restaurant has a timer on the drive-through to track how quickly customers are satisfied. Dangerous diet pills help those who are overweight drop 10 pounds in a week. Credit cards allow us to spend thousands of dollars we haven't yet earned. Crying children are rewarded with electronics and sweets. Of course, unintended consequences result.

The second our children are introduced to this incredible world, immediate satisfaction is a way of life, and it gets in the way of critical thinking skills as well as basic knowledge. Children who understand that a company such as Lego began with a person who believed in an idea and spent years working to create a brand are more likely to succeed.

Will Smith tells about a request his father once made. His dad had recently torn down a brick wall at his business, and he asked his sons to rebuild it better than it was before. Both of the boys said it would be impossible but took on the challenge. It took them a year and a half to rebuild the wall, and from this experience, Smith learned something great.

"You don't set out to build a wall," he recalled. "You don't say 'I'm going to build the biggest, baddest, greatest wall that's ever been built.' You don't start there. You say, 'I'm going to lay this brick as perfectly as a brick can be laid. You do that every single day. And soon you have a wall."

Smith learned that you achieve long-term goals by doing the best job you can today. He began to understand that the small things we do each day, laying one brick at a time, help us accomplish the big goals we set.

If you teach your students to be patient thinkers and creators, they will understand that they can create a bright future for themselves. If you don't do this, if you merely give kids an unlimited supply of entertainment, you will deplete organic opportunities for them to become producers.

Take Timmy. From the moment he was born, every time he cried, Timmy was placed in front of the beautifully bright television to watch cartoons.

As Timmy grew, his teacher played a lot of movies and videos in the classroom but seldom challenged Timmy to create anything for himself.

At Christmas, when Timmy received a new PlayStation, a bright smile grew from one ear to the other. His happiness brought joy to all who saw him.

But soon, Timmy's parents had to yell at him to get him to come to the dinner table. They had to plead with him to shut off the game, help out around the house, and go to bed. They had to force him to go outside and be active.

Up to this point, everything in Timmy's life had been created by someone else and given to him. When one of his "friends" asks if he wants to try drugs, how might Timothy respond? Will he be able to think for himself?

It's hard to say. If Timothy had learned to think independently, work hard, and develop goals, dreams, and ambitions, if he had been encouraged to create instead of to absorb everyone else's beliefs, he just might respond with, "No way" because he knows his future is too valuable to throw away. Instead, it's hard to predict what he'll choose.

We have to teach our students to think. We have to help them understand that by working day in and day out and doing the right thing, they can achieve almost anything. At the same time, we have to stop taking the easy way out when our students throw a fit and say they're bored.

We must stop the trend of superficial thinking and begin developing existential thinkers, goal-oriented children who will become successful adults. Although parents have the most influence on how their children think, there's no question that teachers influence them too.

Strange as it might seem, most of our lower income students don't know what success looks like beyond what they see on television or hear on the radio. It's up to their teachers to show them what goes on behind the scenes because they literally don't know, and if they don't know, how can they be expected to think critically?

Take Disney's hit movie *Frozen*. Children watched it in theatres, on DVDs, and at their friends' homes, and it was impossible to escape the songs. When I asked my students how the movie was made, no one knew.

Answers included, "They just sing songs" and "I think it was Disney."

This was a learning opportunity, a classic teachable moment.

I started by explaining that movies are written just like books, something my students were truly surprised to hear. Once the script was written, I told them, it went through an approval process where a whole series of people decided if, when, and how to turn it into a great movie.

I explained how production companies, writers, agencies, actors, and actresses dedicated thousands of hours to creating the perfect production we saw at the theater. I explained that the movie was filmed in numerous locations, once again with thousands of different camera shots and workers on the production crew.

Then marketing companies got involved. Why? To create previews and commercials that got kids excited about seeing the movie in theaters.

My students were astonished. What a revelation to learn all this!

Not until this lesson did they realize that movies didn't just magically appear. It took hard work and dedication, thousands of hours of planning, hundreds if not thousands of people doing a multitude of different jobs, and sometimes years to produce the films they so adored.

I concluded the lesson by asking my students to brainstorm what type of movies they would like to make and to decide which of their friends would be best for the roles. They also got to decide the locations in which to film.

I wanted to combat the fact that children are constantly entertained and continuously taking in ideas rather than bringing their own ideas to life. We didn't have the wherewithal to film our movies at school, but I encouraged my students to do it at home, and many of them did.

It's our job to teach our students that, rich or poor, they all have the opportunity to create rather than simply consume. Confidence grows when children believe in themselves enough to begin doing this.

You can be the thoughtful teacher who builds generations of happy and thriving families. You can help lower income children become successful adults who permanently leave poverty behind.

My fellow teachers, encourage your students through each and every activity to think independently. Good things will follow.

CHAPTER 15:

A LESSON FROM LAUREN ON BUILDING STRONG WOMEN

If you are not fully utilizing half the talent in the country,
you are not going to get too close to the top.

Bill Gates

I've taught many third, fourth, and fifth grade girls who are as academically successful or more successful than their male classmates.

In my experience, female students at young ages seem to have more maturity, a stronger work ethic, and the ability to grasp higher level concepts than their male counterparts.

Yet as middle school approaches, many girls stop performing at such high levels. The number of highly successful girls suddenly declines and males take the lead, excelling academically and eventually moving into more highly paid careers.

Why does this happen? How does this happen? And what can we do about it?

Imagining all the incredible female students who have walked through my classroom but failed to live up to their potential breaks my heart.

The most creative student I ever taught had the characteristics of a CEO, but she seldom spoke a word and usually kept to herself. She made bracelets, necklaces, food, books, and origami, and her to-do list never stopped. Her creativity and ability to sustain productivity and keep up with gifted and talented homework requirements all while traveling back and forth between her divorced parents was inspiring.

One day, she finished her work early and dropped it off at my desk.

"Never stop producing," I told her. "Look around at your classmates. We all have talents, but not one person in this room, including me, has your ability to create such amazing art!"

She perked up and smiled. This was a clear boost to her confidence.

"Even more amazing is how much you enjoy what you're doing. It doesn't even seem like work to you. Keep doing what you love. Keep on producing. There will always be opportunities to get paid for doing what you love!" My goal was to convince her of her worth in the hopes that she'd keep excelling beyond elementary school.

The talented young lady continued the conversation, "Thanks, Mr. Duncan. This weekend I made $60.00."

I laughed out loud. This girl was relentless. And she'd spoken! "And how did you come to make this $60.00?"

"Lemonade stand. I set it up at the front of the street and parents loved it," she replied.

Her classmates were still working on the assignment, so I took the opportunity to talk to this young lady about college. I shared the scary statistics showing bright young girls falling behind boys academically and how most women are paid less than men who are doing the same job.

"If you want something," I told her, "you have the ability to go out and get it. You don't have to rely on anyone else to get that Mercedes you see driving down the street. Envision yourself driving it when you grow up. You won't have to wait until Christmas to buy that Louis Vuitton bag you like so much because you'll be able to afford to buy it yourself. You deserve to be great."

Recognizing the talents of our students is not enough. We must teach them how to use their gifts to reach a higher quality of life, and we must have the same high expectations for our young ladies that we do for our young men.

Lauren's Metamorphosis

The school bell rang at 7:45 a.m. sharp. At 8:00 a.m., an in-class breakfast was served. Kids ranging in age from nine to 10 began chatting. The boys' topic was their favorite anime characters. Student's voices could be heard saying, "Goku is my favorite," "Batman can defeat them all!," and "Spiderman is the best!"

The girls talked about hairstyles. I heard things like, "Mom straightened my hair" and "My sister does her hair with a braid to the side" and "Oooh, I like your hair today!" Chuckles burst out when Zachorian joined the girls, saying, "My mom's hair fell out!"

In the middle of it all, like an owl resting quietly in its tree, elegantly unnoticed, Lauren started her morning work. Eating breakfast at home gave her a head start, and she took advantage of it. By contrast, especially in the beginning of the year, her peers wouldn't have dreamed of starting an assignment without the teacher telling them to.

Lauren didn't speak. Not even a peep. It's easy to get a read on most students within minutes of meeting them, but not her. Lauren kept to herself.

"How are you doing?" I asked her.

"Fine, thank you," she replied.

"Do you need any assistance with the bell ringer?"

"No thank you," Lauren responded.

I let her know that if she needed help to please raise her hand.

My mind began to race, thinking about Lauren's interactions with other students and staff, or the lack thereof. My classroom was an active, high-paced, connected environment that encouraged collaboration with fellow students, so why didn't Lauren speak to anyone?

Just 15 minutes later, breakfast and daily announcements were over. Students cleaned up their areas, threw away trash, and began their bell ringers. Lauren had already finished. Her four questions were organized and answered. She sat quietly as

I scanned her work. It was a perfect 100! I had a thinker, some-one who was exceptionally smart and ready to excel academically. I gave her a multiplication worksheet referencing correct answers to letters. She used the letters to create phrases that matched the illustration at the bottom of the worksheet. While she challenged herself with advanced activities, I assisted other students. An hour quickly passed, and her class was dismissed and rotated to their other teacher.

This was the first week of school. I was taking my first steps toward my goal of creating self-recognized greatness in each and every one of these young human beings. So far Lauren was quiet, shy, and sharp. Now she needed to be encouraged to go to the top of the mountain of success, to discover her talents, and to use them to make herself and everyone around her better. She had just begun her journey to greatness.

The Creative

Riiiiing. The bell burst out its monotonous and loud tune. We were now a few weeks into the school year, and routines were becoming smooth and natural. As always, Lauren finished her work early and raised her hand.

I approached her desk, knelt my 6'6 frame gingerly next to her chair, and asked, "How may I help you, Lauren?"

"Can I work on my bracelets?" she asked softly and hesitantly.

Seeing that she was beyond meeting my expectations in the classroom and this was her first request of the year, I responded with, "I don't see why not!"

To my surprise, she immediately reached into her pencil bag and pulled out a large concoction of multi-colored plastic lacing. I walked away but kept an eye on her. Her hands weaved colorful plastic with precision and speed. Ten minutes passed, and I was thoroughly impressed.

"Wow, Lauren! You are truly awesome; how did you learn to make this?" I asked.

Her response was as simple as it gets.

"I watched it on the internet."

While most students sat at home playing video games, eating junk food, or watching movies, one of them was actually doing beneficial research and widening her skills and talents.

I watched as she pulled out a small metal clip, tied the remaining sections of the strings around it, and held it up towards me. She then said, "This one is for you, Mr. Duncan!"

With a smile on my face, I gave her a sincere thank you for creating a handmade gift just for me.

That evening after school, I went to work out at my local gym. The only items I took with me were my wireless headphones and car keys so I could avoid the hassle of getting a locker. The front desk of the gym had the courtesy to hold your keys while you worked out, putting them in a container with several other sets. As I turned in my keys, a bell went off in my head. Lauren's bright orange plastic lace would become part of my key chain and easily distinguish it from all the other sets.

Sure enough, after that, each time I started walking towards the exit, a staff member would grab my keys and hand them to me, saying, "Hope you had a good workout. Have a great day, Mr. Duncan." Lauren's gift made my day a little easier.

Albert Einstein said, "Everybody is a genius, but if you judge a fish on its ability to climb a tree, it will live its whole life believing it is stupid." Our leaders have created a curriculum that is supposed to benefit all children by giving them the tools to be successful future citizens. Unfortunately, we too often lose focus on the child as an individual. We mold students into a system, expecting them to all be the same, forgetting each and every child is different.

As the year continued, I learned more about Lauren. She realized I was sincerely interested in helping her reach her full potential. She knew I cared about what was going on at school and at home, and therefore it was easier for her to feel comfortable sharing with me. She trusted me.

Blessed to have two hard-working parents, her work ethic was undeniable, and I'm sure we could give most if not all the credit to her parents. Nonetheless, it was gratifying to see her transformation from a quiet student who didn't know how to express her strengths to someone who would go on to influence her entire grade level. Of all my students, she experienced the most interpersonal growth.

The Adult in a Child

One day after school as we were waiting for her mom to pick her up, Lauren told me her cousin was living with them. She said he'd moved in a couple weeks ago because her uncle was making really bad decisions and had gone to jail.

Lauren said, "I kept telling him he needs to stop drinking all those beers, but he didn't listen. It's really sad. You know, if I had a nickel for every one of those cans, I might be rich!"

At a young age, she had a wisdom far deeper than those around her. As quiet as she was in class, she had the confidence to tell adults how to make the right decisions.

The Businesswoman

Each day, Lauren shared her unique creations and I pushed her to understand math and business. We spoke about how some students held bake sales or sold lemonade to raise money. She could save up money, work on her crafts and, when the time was right, start her own business.

Sadly, most students from inner city lower income schools never hear such encouraging words. I wanted to make sure Lauren knew she could do it, and indeed, she did. Her key chains became popular throughout the entire school. As if this wasn't cool enough, she expanded her product line and began making purses out of used clothes and recycled clothing. She would cut the clothing into perfect shapes and sew them together, using her sewing machine for the tight stitching and her hands for the larger knots. The bags included outside compartments, inside pockets, and sturdy straps you could easily throw over your shoulder.

Watching Lauren's business unfold was fascinating. A nine-year-old girl was creating products independently and inspiring her friends to do the same. She began inviting classmates to her home on the weekends and showing them the step-by-step process of making purses and key chains. She was making connections and making a difference!

The student who used to hold her head down, the one who didn't speak unless spoken to, didn't exist anymore. She was now a leader, and her work and confidence spoke for themselves. I was no longer the only one talking to her. All her classmates were talking to her, asking questions and making comments like, "Can you make me a purse?" "I want a blue key chain," and "Come on, Lauren, be in our group."

Thank goodness she handled the "paparazzi" well and wasn't overwhelmed by the sudden demands. Her peers were watching her every step, and she was a great candidate for the position. Her work ethic positively impacted them all, and she wasn't finished.

The Musician

Every day after lunch, our grade level had up to 15 minutes for recess. Lauren always hung around the teachers for mature conversation while a few of her friends tagged along.

"Do you like music, Mr. Duncan," she asked one day.

"Why, of course," I answered. "We always have it playing in class, don't we?"

Our classroom speakers often played Mozart, a string quartet, or Jack Johnson. The first time I put music on, I asked my students how it related to what we were learning and gave a short lesson on rhythm, concluding with, "If you listen close, you can find a pattern in every song!"

Lauren told me she took piano lessons and really loved music. I asked if she could tell me how music related to school and what we were studying.

She replied, "Music is rhythm, and in math, we learn to recognize patterns."

"Wow! Music is indeed full of patterns. I am impressed you remember!"

"I wrote a song of my own, Mr. Duncan. Would you like to hear it?"

I was filled with joy. "Let's hear it," I said.

Let me remind you, this was the same girl who once upon a time could have been mistaken as mute. Now she was out of her shell. She brought two of her friends over and they teamed up. This was going to be a performance of a lifetime, right here on a hundred-degree day, as the sun waved its eerie reflective halo on the asphalt.

With one student on her left and the other on her right, Lauren whispered directions. Her friends held their arms connected above her and released them as Lauren walked through the opening gate of hands and began to sing.

"When I go out into the world to find something new, I need someone to guide me, someone to guide me through, and that person is you."

As if all the angels in heaven were singing, her two friends joined in harmony, "Come out of the dark dark dark side, come out of the dark dark dark side, I need you!"

The harmony stopped and Lauren continued, "So let's go out in the world and see, the world is full of mysteries, so come out of the dark dark dark side, come out of the dark dark dark side."

Her crew joined in again, "Come out of the dark dark dark side. You are the only one who can guide me through."

Lauren then sang, "Come out of the dark," and her friends repeated, "dark dark dark side." Her two friends picked her up in the air in celebration as she gave a final bow.

My hands clapping in proud applause, I stood in disbelief. Without knowing it, Lauren had just reached greatness. As she smiled and responded to the compliments, a glow of confidence clearly showed on her face. Step by step, Lauren had learned to channel her talents into productivity and connectivity with others. She became something greater than I had envisioned. I even learned a lesson myself—do not put a cap on how much you think someone can grow.

In hindsight, Lauren didn't have a powerful influence on others on the second day of school. It took the entire year! She had some successes and also some failures. As Michael Jordan said, "I have failed over and over and over again in my life, and that is why I succeed."

The greatest teachers not only teach students valuable skills and life lessons but also they teach students how to teach themselves. Lauren now had the tools to continue her passions, look her fears in the eye, and continue climbing the ladder to success. This shy reserved girl went through a metamorphosis, transforming into a shining light who influenced everyone around her. The most beautiful part was that she had the type of personality that would pay it forward.

Every student who walks through school is a true miracle. In this world of almost eight billion people, no two people are exactly the same. We all have strengths and weaknesses, struggles and talents, interests and dislikes. We must learn to embrace our rarity and the fact that we are all different. The greatest teachers help their students become smarter academically *and* help them develop the confidence they need to overcome their weaknesses.

Of the 50 students I had that year, each and every one of them had a unique talent. I took some time towards the end of the year to write each child a personal letter. The following is the letter I wrote to Lauren.

Lauren,

You have been such a gift to our classroom this year. I have learned just as much from you as you have learned from me. Your creative mind is an incredible talent. In addition, you are kind to everyone around you, sharing your gifts with them. Find what you enjoy doing in life and continue doing it to the best of your ability. Be great and shoot for the stars even if the person next to you isn't doing the same. You deserve greatness, and it is up to you to achieve it. I know you will choose the right path! Remember, we create our own luck. I'm excited to see what you will be doing when you are my age.

Mr. Duncan

New Era

It has been nearly 200 years since Harriet Tubman proved her worth. Any woman who escapes slavery to turn around and risk it all saving more than 300 people is a hero. Oprah Winfrey created a billion-dollar, with a capital B, enterprise. Hilary Clinton ran for president of the United States.

Times have changed. Encourage your female students to soar beyond society's expectations. Tell them you believe in them. Show them role models of successful women they can emulate. Work to imbue in them the strength and confidence they need to achieve and excel.

It's a new era, and it's time for women of all ages to be recognized for how great they are.

CHAPTER 16:

FEAR, SELF-CONTROL, AND LEARNING TO STAY SAFE

I believe that we are solely responsible for our choices, and we have to accept the consequences of every deed, word, and thought throughout our lifetime.

Elisabeth Kubler-Ross

The way children are disciplined at home can impact how they respond in the classroom.

Some parents curse and yell at their children. When a teacher asks young boys or girls from such an environment to please stop talking to their neighbor, they seldom take the request seriously. Other households discipline by taking away toys, videos games, or other privileges.

Still other parents find themselves assigning chores and yard work to ensure their child doesn't misbehave again.

In our household, Grandma always worked. She stood on her feet all day checking groceries only to come home to cooking, doing laundry, and getting us ready for bed. My brothers and I didn't know what chores were. Grandpa was aging, developing a shorter temper each day, and struggling to keep up with three hyper children. It didn't help that he was a diabetic and living with extreme pain. This mostly kind and loving man sometimes struggled to find the best way to discipline his grandchildren.

I vividly remember how Grandpa wanted to be able to hear every word uttered by the reporters on the evening news. I liked to play in the living room making banging noises on the floor with my toy cars while using my mouth to create sound effects as I drove up and down the furniture and walls.

"Shut up!" Grandpa would sometimes yell, scaring me and causing my heart to race. The loud screaming worsened as he aged. Grandma's hearing was poor, so she didn't intervene. After repeating himself once or twice, his impatience could get the best of him. He would scream at the top of his lungs, his face so red I thought he was going to have a heart attack.

All the locals knew him as the mechanic who could fix just about anything or the carpenter who could make just about anything. He was always fixing or building new things for the truck or the house. As much as I loved being outside, I never spent much time with Grandpa.

"Josh, hand me the Phillips," he would say.

Not knowing what that was but too afraid to ask, I would grab the first tool I saw.

"I said the Phillips; don't you know what the Phillips is?" he would scream as loudly as he could.

I never learned much about Grandpa's tools because I was too afraid to make a mistake. I quickly became a grandma's boy and joined her in the kitchen or played outside, staying far away from my grandpa's work. Most of the time he was kind, happy to teach, and supportive, yet his impatient moments stuck out more than the others and created a lasting fear.

Both my dad and my grandpa shared a terrible habit. Whenever their buttons were pushed and I was in range, I would get a strong slap on the back of my head. This was different from a spanking because I never saw it coming. The shock of a hand hitting the back of my head hurt more than being screamed at. It hurt physically, and it also hurt emotionally.

Still, this was the same grandpa who would wake up when I had nightmares and make my tears go away, the same grandpa who would sit up with me when my legs were cramping and give me a massage.

It didn't help his mood when Grandpa began to have trouble getting up and down from his chair. Whenever I saw that he was about to lose his temper, I would dart up as fast as I could and run into the yard. I learned this was the smartest method. He rarely chased me outside, and my absence gave him the opportunity to calm down.

Grandpa's most efficient discipline started with the simple phrase, "Go pick out your switch." This only happened when I made a mistake three times. Three strikes and I was out. Like a guilty dog with its tail between its legs, I'd slowly walk from the living room through our connected garage to our back yard and finally to the young tree that had dozens of switches to pick from.

"Let me see," I always thought to myself. "I could pick the smallest and thinnest stick but those sting the most. I could pick the heaviest stick and prevent the sting but the weight will make the blow much harder. I could pick the stick right in the middle and get the best of both worlds. Or more like the worst of both worlds!"

This thought process gave me time to think about why I was in trouble and how I could prevent it from happening again. Believe me, I rarely repeated the same mistake four times.

When grandparents are responsible for bringing up their grandchildren, it can have lasting effects on everyone. My upbringing was challenging, but it didn't come close to the hardships some children face. Ninety percent of the time, my grandparents provided a home filled with love and happiness. At a young age, I understood that Mom was not there for me. I understood that Dad was not a role model. I understood that my grandma and grandpa were everything that everyone else was not. Even in their old age and impoverished state of living, all that mattered was knowing I had someone to trust. I felt love. It was better than the short times spent living with my parents or stepparents, times of violence and alcohol I would rather not discuss.

My grandparents were great because they took initiative. They embraced the responsibility of raising their grandchildren, putting clothes on their backs, providing food at the table, and making sure they made it to school for a good education.

They also had a controlling side when it came to raising us. This was an outgrowth of seeing so many people make bad decisions and knowing that if they stuck to doing it their way, things would be okay. Sometimes, though, their way felt overbearing.

I walked into the kitchen in my Looney Toons pajamas one morning ready to fill my hungry morning tummy with breakfast. Milk and cereal would most definitely hit the spot. I took the initiative because who wants to have to wait for their grandparents to pour them a bowl of cereal when they can do it themselves?

I opened up the fridge and grabbed the nearly full gallon of milk with one hand wrapped around the handle and the other hand supporting the bottom of the jug. The next step was to grab the cereal on top of the refrigerator.

This was not the easiest task. I couldn't reach the top, but that didn't stop me. One hop, and my bottom landed on the cabinet.

Another hop up, and I grabbed the cereal from the top of the fridge and put it on the cabinet, where I gingerly sat back on my bottom and scooted off onto the floor.

I had successfully retrieved the milk and cereal without help from Grandma or Grandpa! Piece of cake from here.

My ninja turtle cereal bowl with an attached straw from which to drink the remaining sugar-flavored milk was easy access in the drying rack. Right next to it was a spoon.

I checked off the steps. "Cereal poured in awesome ninja turtle bowl. No word from Grandma in her bedroom. No word from Grandpa in the living room."

Due to the weight of the milk and the height of our table, it seemed easiest to let the jug stay on the table as I began pouring. Slowly and carefully, the milk began to smoothly stream into the center of the bowl. Just as the bowl was nearly full, the bottom of the jug slid out from the table and landed on the edge of the bowl, causing milk to spill all over the table and drain onto my shirt.

I panicked. I didn't want to get yelled at and disappoint my grandpa. I didn't want Grandma to have to clean it up when I knew she was getting ready for a full day at work.

In a rush, I grabbed two towels from the kitchen and quickly swiped, grabbed, and sponged all the milk from the table. After shaking all the loose cereal into the trash, I threw the towels into the dirty laundry and quickly returned to finish off the little cereal I had left.

That day at school, I started to smell something strange. Looking around, I scanned my friends to see who was producing this horrid sour smell. That's when I noticed my friends were pointing at me.

I reached down, grabbed my shirt with two hands, and pulled it up to my nose to get a good whiff.

Bad idea. The smell immediately made me gag. Approaching my teacher, I told her how I'd spilled milk on my white shirt but didn't change it because it hadn't stained. She didn't hesitate to let me go to the nurse to change into a new shirt.

Innocent accidents didn't always turn out so well. We were never allowed to make a mistake. If something spilled, screaming and scolding followed. The pressure of being perfect sometimes caused me to perform badly in high pressure situations.

Once I became a teacher, I used my experiences and hard-won wisdom to empower my students.

It was incredible to see their faces when they spilled milk or juice in the classroom. Usually, they looked as if they'd seen a ghost. Fear would overcome them and they'd look at me as if I were about to scream with fury.

Instead, I'd surprise them with a smile. "It's okay," I'd say. "Accidents happen. They're how we get better and more responsible. Please clean up your mess without distracting the rest of the class."

Their friends usually clamored to help, but I didn't allow this because it would become a distraction and take away from learning that it's okay to make a mistake as long as you take the responsibility for fixing it.

It's truly rewarding to relive your childhood through your students and have the wisdom to change the mistakes your elders made. Those mistakes were most likely the same mistakes their parents made, and I found it empowering to break the chain not only for myself but for my students. It was priceless to see the look of delight on the faces of empowered children. Knowing they would likely pass this same lesson on to their children was evidence I was changing the world.

This matters because how people think influences their odds of success. When the greatest athletes are in the last seconds of a tied championship game, do they think about how they're going to win the game or how they're going to lose it? Great athletes envision goals, touchdowns, baskets, and home runs. If you want your children to do something well, are you going to tell them, "Don't drop the glass," "Don't drop the phone," or "Don't spill the milk"?

Ironically, this is often how we speak to our students when we want them to be careful. The problem is, such words unintentionally set them up for failure. Instead, we can set our children up for success by rephrasing our words, something like, "I know how careful you are, and that's why I know you'll be responsible with the glass you're carrying. I'm impressed with how many times you've poured your own glass of milk. I'm proud of you." Affirming them can increase their confidence and empower them to complete their day-to-day tasks with fewer mistakes.

The way children are raised also has a significant impact on the adults they become. As teachers, we cannot change what happens in the homes of our students. What we do have control over is what happens in our classrooms. Creating an environment that challenges students allows plenty of mistakes to occur. Without opportunities to make mistakes, how can they learn to be responsible, especially if their home environments create fear? Embrace an active classroom environment and know that you can be a big reason your students become confident and independent adults.

Fear

Fear can never be defined by a single thing or event. Fear is relative to each individual and the situations they face. You already know I'm afraid of spiders, but they fascinated my student John.

Often, fear lies in the unknown. Even though an itsy bitsy spider could make the man students called "Gigantè" scream in a high-pitched voice, I never took the time to learn more about them. Consequently, I'm still scared of spiders today, and the same thing usually holds true for how we feel about people who are different from us.

The quote "The fear lies in my lack of awareness of the other side. Today I know that we are the same, you and I. Different kind of skin, different set of eyes, two different minds, but only one God," sums it up well.

Many people believe childhood fears become imbedded in our DNA and haunt us for the rest of our lives. What can we do to help students avoid the negative effects that come along with fear?

I vividly remember the original Nintendo game system. Duck Hunter was my favorite. Who would have imagined it would be possible to point your plastic gun at a television, especially in the '90s, and shoot ducks crossing the screen?

My brother's favorite game was Mario. He would jump on top of each level through hidden tricks and skip the same levels it took me hours to complete. I always made it to the final world, but I could never defeat Bowser and rescue the princess. It was my habit to watch as my brother saved her dozens of times. One particular evening, he made it to the princess, his eyes glued to the screen with the focus Nolan Ryan had in the 1969 World Series.

I needed to run to the bathroom, but I wanted to make it back before he got to Bowser and saved the princess once again, so I quickly jumped past the TV, my sole intention to avoid distracting his game play.

Unfortunately, my plan backfired. I made a clear landing on the other side, but my weight caused a small bounce on the ground, and the overheated Nintendo suddenly reset. My terrified eyes fearfully connected with my brother's, and before I knew it, everything was a blur.

Waking up from what felt like a dream, I lay in his arms with his hand behind my head. Sharp pain began to pulsate down the side of my face, and tears started rolling down my cheeks. Enraged, lost in the moment, my big brother had knocked me out cold only to regret his reaction after realizing he'd seriously hurt me.

I still remember him walking me to the kitchen to get ice and my nearly seven-foot-tall uncle suspiciously asking, "What happened?"

As my brother stammered out his words, I quickly interjected, "I jumped across the TV screen trying to avoid messing up the video game and fell and hit the wall."

Thankfully, that was the last time my brother seriously hurt me, at least on purpose, but the incident left me with uncertainty as to what could possibly happen next and created an anxiety of the unknown.

Speaking of my brother, half a mile down the road from my house was a park hosting the city's most competitive pick-up basketball games. The competition was great, but a recent drive-by shooting and separate knife attack plus drugs and gambling had made this park unsafe. I was only eight, and the one time I went against my grandpa's orders and went there to play, he put a belt to my hind end and reiterated that I was to never step foot in the park again. After that, I walked across the street and played basketball at the local church. My grandparents could see me, and at suppertime, I could hear my grandpa's loud shout.

Each Wednesday, the church held evening services. The basketball court was on the backside of the church, and never once did a member ask me not to play during those hours.

One day, my brother walked up with determination in his step. I assumed he was going to offer to shoot around with me until I noticed he had a beanie in his hand. He said he was going to run into the church and be right out. I replied, "Okay, I'll just be here." He gave me a look that struck fear in my heart when he said, "I'm going to run in and back out, and when I run out, you are going to run with me as fast as you can!"

What I thought was a beanie turned out to be a ski mask with holes cut out for eyes. I watched as my brother put the beanie on, pulled out a bag, and ran into the church just as they were taking the offering. He snatched the plates of money and threw them into his bag and seconds later sprinted back out the door, pulling me along as I struggled to keep up. I followed him to my elementary school's air conditioning units. I still remember him pulling out a stack of money and offering me a portion. Even at a young age, I knew it was wrong. I refused to take anything, but how was I to digest these bizarre events I could neither anticipate nor avoid, especially when my own family member was committing them?

My young mind then had to compare my brothers and parents with the same two men who robbed my grandma as she walked out of her grocery store after a hard day's work. They came inches from running her over and ripped her purse off her shoulder, escaping with the little money she'd made. Maybe they needed it more than we did. Maybe they didn't know that money was putting food on the table for the grandkids she was raising. Maybe they had kids who were hungry themselves. But the truth is, they probably didn't.

I was often afraid, but one thing was for sure. In spite of all the aggressive things my brother did, he had my back. My grandparents and aunts would go watch my cousin play baseball while I rushed off to play games such as kickball, dodgeball, and wall ball with other kids at the park. Our games were unorganized and lacked parental supervision. Naturally, this left room for bullying. During a game of wall ball one day, a kid much bigger than me decided to throw the ball at my face even after I touched the wall and was safe. Instead of checking on me and apologizing for not following the rules, he made fun of me and laughed.

My big brother saw the entire thing. As he walked over, I already felt sorry for this kid, as there was nothing I could do to help him. Within seconds, he and my brother were rolling on the ground and he was bleeding from his mouth and nose. My brother grabbed me and we quickly walked away from the commotion.

Whether it was fighting for me or for pride, it seemed like the fights never stopped. After several mishaps at school, numerous suspensions, and several arrests, my brother was required to attend an alternative school. I never understood why the teens who needed the most supervision had to wait at the same bus stop without any adults in the area.

Watching from across the street, I saw four teens surround my brother. He took the first swing and jumped on top of the smallest guy in the gang. A few punches in, and blood began staining the white uniform shirts of both fighters. That is, until the other teens started kicking, punching, and overpowering my brother until his white shirt was completely covered in a fresh pool of blood. My grandpa finally ran across the street and broke up the fight, but I thought my brother was going to die. Why couldn't he see that this vicious cycle would never stop? By taking vengeance on one person, you created a completely new battle with 10 others.

It all climaxed with a report in the newspaper about my brother's best friend. The headline said, "Houston teen shot execution style on school track." These and many other experiences informed how I responded to my own students who got into fights. The fact was, I was fearful for them. They weren't going to stay fourth graders forever.

One day at recess, two of my students were arguing over what one thought was a touchdown and the other said wasn't, and Hector's trash talk struck a nerve. Angry, feeling cheated, Matthew swiped as quick as he could at the football only to catch Hector's face. Tempers flared, and in an attempt to prevent the aggression from going any further, I ran over and separated them, repeating, "Stop! Please calm down!" Instead, they slipped past my grip and tackled one another before I pulled them apart.

"Are you kidding me?" I asked. "I told you to stop! Now both of you, two best friends, have to be written up and sent to the principal's office, and I don't even have a choice."

Overwhelming emotions and reality set in as both students started crying. Two of my classroom leaders were embarrassed as they looked down, avoiding eye contact with their classmates who were now watching with great attention.

After all was said and done, the boys made up and apologized to one another. It was understandable that two nine-year-old best friends got flustered and fought over a game. The problem was their inability to control themselves even after I came between them.

What if these two great students ran into someone who had nothing to lose? What if my students found themselves at a basketball park in high school and decided it was okay to do the same thing to someone who wasn't their best friend but was carrying a knife or a gun? I took the opportunity to talk to them about recognizing their surroundings, but instead of scolding and screaming, I complimented them.

I told them, "Hector and Matthew, I understand you really care about winning, and that's a great spirit to have, especially in sports. You need to have a winning spirit and give it all you've got." By saying this, I gained their trust and also their attention. Then I added, "You also need to understand who you're dealing with. If you did that in a real game, you would be suspended and then your team would lose its best players! Is that a great idea?"

Both students simultaneously responded, "No, sir."

"What if this wasn't your best friend?" I continued. "You know how many crazy and illogical people are in this world? I've seen it firsthand, people who are angry and don't care how bright your future is. If you got in a fight with them, you could be seriously hurt or even killed. You're way too great to fight over a game. You have such bright futures, and you're going to go way further than anybody trying to knock you off course!"

They were now looking at each other and nodding with smiles on their faces.

"Last but not least," I told them, "never go past me when I get in between you and tell you to stop. If you were my children, I would have grabbed you both and lifted you up in the air and you wouldn't even be able to touch each other!"

The conversation finished with another "Yes, sir" and chuckles. Their parents were already disciplining these students at home in addition to reprimands they were receiving in the principal's office. I didn't need to say or do anything more.

I was able to take the lessons I learned watching my brother go down the wrong road and apply them to numerous elementary school incidents. Perhaps I needed to see that side of the world, that side of people, in order to truly impact students who were going through similar incidents. There is never a better time to teach a child about the dangers of the world than in the teachable moment. I wanted my students to learn this information from me, their teacher, before they could be involved in an incident in real life that could put their lives on the line.

CHAPTER 17:

WHAT ON EARTH
ARE YOU EATING?

It is health that is real wealth and not pieces of gold and silver.

Mahatma Gandhi

"Mr. Duncan, Mr. Duncan, Mr. Duncan! Can we have snack yet?"

The question caught on like a California wildfire. Doritos started popping out of hats, Fruit Roll-Ups rolled out of desks, fruit juices and sodas appeared from backpacks. It was truly astonishing to witness.

Having lived through malnutrition, I knew that eating habits strongly influence young lives, so I recognized the problem very quickly. I made an announcement. "From now on, you may only bring healthy foods for snack time in my class."

You would think they'd just received the news that they'd never again have another second of recess. Grunts and frustrated mumbles spread through the classroom.

Taking something away from people without explaining why is risky. It isn't always easy to explain "why," but it's usually worth the effort, so I gave it a try.

"Wow, look at this bottle of Coke." I held up a bottle and used an excited voice, interrupting the work at hand. It was just a week after my "healthy foods during snack time" announcement, and all eyes were on me.

"Let's take a look at what it's made of. I'm sure, no, I'm positive, it has ingredients we've all heard of." Sarcasm danced on my tongue. "Hmm, here it is, right here on the back." I pointed to the nutritional label. "High fructose corn syrup. I've heard of syrup, but high fructose corn? What in the world could that be?"

I allowed some students to take a jab at it, and no one was even close.

I went on, "Caramel color and phosphoric acid…You mean they add a color to the soda? What is this stuff? How is this possible?"

My students were baffled, so I shared a science experiment I'd done in my early school years. "Did you guys know that if you put a rusty penny in a cup of Coke and let it soak overnight, the penny will be clean and shiny in the morning? The Coke eats away all the dirt and grime and rust. Imagine what it's doing inside of you! Does this make you think about soda a little differently?"

After recess that morning, I lined the students up and said, "We're going to do a little experiment before we go back inside." I shook a can of soda, tossed it high into the sky, and threw it towards some rocks a little distance away. It was a perfect shot. The can punctured in one spot and began gushing like Spindletop, the first major gusher of the Texas oil boom. The children screamed in excitement.

"Can I ask you all a question?" I said rhetorically. "Does water do this when you shake it up and throw it?"

Every head shook no.

"Then I wonder why we're so quick to put something this explosive in our stomachs."

Overwhelming a child with too much information all at once is also risky. This was the last thing I wanted to do with a full day of teaching ahead, so we wrapped up the quick lesson on soda and headed back into the classroom.

A week or so later, I gave my next healthy food lesson with the help of Takis, a rolled corn tortilla chip in the shape of a French fry. Kids love these things, but they're anything but healthy.

"Wow, cool, Takis! Remember, we should know each ingredient in our food, right?" I pointed to the list of ingredients and began reading the common ingredients such as salt, sugar, and corn flour. Then I paused.

"What about these ingredients? Artificial flavoring…Who knows what artificial means?"

A student raised her hand and answered, "It means fake."

"That's right. Okay, here we have monosodium glutamate, maltodextrin, sodium diacetate. Do these sound like items we buy at the store? I wonder why they're in our food? What are these things?"

The next ingredients really triggered the students' interest. "Artificial coloring, fd&c red no. 40 lake, fd&c yellow no. 6 lake. Are you telling me they're putting fake color in the chips you're eating? No wonder your fingers are red after eating them!"

As the year played on, I often took quick breaks to talk about the ingredients in common unhealthy snacks. We spoke about how many of the ingredients in our food are created in a chemical lab by scientists and why they aren't good for us. We paid special attention to high fructose corn syrup since it appears in so much of our food and is linked to so many serious health issues.

One day, a parent emailed me asking for clarification after her daughter mentioned that she wasn't allowed to bring a popular brand of juice box to school in her lunch box anymore. I emailed her back with the product information, concluding, "It's truly up to you guys. We've done some activities in the classroom learning about the foods we eat, and this brand of juice box happens to have high fructose corn syrup. I am very complimentary of her snack and lunch on the other hand!

The parent emailed me back, "We will be more selective in her beverage choices going forward. Thank you, Mr. Duncan. This is why we like you."

As the year wound down, I couldn't believe my eyes. I had stopped discussing ingredients, but students were continuing to gather in groups to analyze the ingredients in their snacks on their own. They were surprised when they discovered a favorite, Sunny Delight, had very little nutritional value and only a small percentage of juice.

Questions and comments came my way, such as, "Why would companies put this stuff in our foods when they know it's bad for us?" and "I'm going to go home and throw away all my mom's soda!" I made sure to warn them they probably shouldn't cross that line. Eventually, 90% of my class was bringing fruits and vegetables for snack time!

It's a proud moment when young people learn how to assess what they're eating and make healthy choices. People do not just eat unhealthy foods because they want to become overweight and sick. The answer lies in knowledge, and knowledge is power.

Most students and adults do not know what we're fueling our bodies with. In a funny way, our bodies are just like the vehicles we drive. Do you want to fill up with a cheap gunk fuel that will severely hinder the vehicle's use, or do you want to fill up with the cleanest and most superior energy possible? To ensure a smooth drive and long life, put healthy foods in your body.

It's great to ask our students to eat well the day before a test because it will make them more focused, but it's empowering to teach them healthy habits throughout the entire year that will impact the rest of their lives.

CHAPTER 18:

GUIDANCE, PARENTAL
AND OTHERWISE

Character cannot be developed in ease and quiet.
Only through experience of trial and suffering can the soul be
strengthened, ambition inspired, and success achieved.

Helen Keller

Do you consider yourself protective? If your children were under the age of 10, would you let them leave the front yard unsupervised? Would you let them leave the neighborhood unsupervised?

Several students in my classroom reminded me of my young self. Every day before and after school, their walk home was more than a mile. They arrived at their apartments after a hard day of school only to look after their younger siblings until their mom, who was single, returned from her evening shift.

Nine-year-olds, taking on adult responsibilities.

When I was a kid, my grandpa always made sure I told him where I was going. My favorite destination was the house of my second grade classmate just two blocks away. Here, Jake and I played videos games and sports and even climbed trees. Most of it was harmless fun. Most of it was also unsupervised. His parents were always locked away in their bedroom.

In a large open field across from his house, we played the most memorable soccer games. There weren't too many rules. If you scored between the two tree branches that lay parallel to one another, your team won. The field was open to the public, and occasionally we found ourselves playing against middle schoolers.

Sprinting down the field one day with the soccer ball directly in front of him and the opportunity to score a goal, Jake pulled his leg back, getting ready to kick the ball as hard as he could. Before his kicking foot reached the forward motion, he was completely blindsided from behind.

The older teenager purposely kicked both of Jake's legs out from under him.

As Jake flew through the air in what seemed slow motion, everyone on the field stopped in shock.

When I saw Jake lying on the ground, hurt and crying, I ran over. Before I could make it to him, he popped up like a jack-in-the-box and began swinging wildly at the bully only to be punched as hard as he'd been kicked. I couldn't just stand there and let my friend get hurt. I jumped in and grabbed the bigger kid by his neck, wrestling him to the ground.

In the dirtiest move of all time, this kid reached into an ant pile, grabbed a handful of dirt and ants, and threw it in my eyes followed by a solid blow of his fist to the side of my head, then left with his friend before we could find help.

Although we were bruised, battered, and lucky to make it out of the situation without serious injuries, Jake and I felt a sense of pride. We had lost, but we had stood up to bullies! We had also learned a valuable lesson. Do not play with older kids without adult supervision.

My experiences gave me a realistic perspective when hearing stories about bullies. I taught my students to fight only as a last resort. I taught them that being proactive can sometimes prevent problems. I taught them to walk together in groups and not to linger after school. I taught them to have their phones ready in case they needed to call an adult, something we didn't have 20 years ago. I taught them to always tell a parent or adult as soon as any sign of bullying appeared.

One year my fifth graders were struggling to get along well with one another. Bullying was common and students were constantly arguing. In a desperate effort to put out the fire before it blazed out of control, the administration decided to place the majority of the misbehaving students in my homeroom section. Apparently 6'6 Mr. Duncan was the magic answer. Unfortunately, the struggles continued.

One day, in desperation, I took blank sheets of paper and ripped them into 25 equal pieces. I gave a piece to each student and instructed, "Using the protection of your desk folder to ensure privacy, I want you to write down the most hurtful thing that has been said or done to you this year. Do not write your name on this paper. I repeat, do not write your name on it. When you're finished, crumple it into a ball, and I'll come around and put it in my bucket."

Once each slip of paper was in the bucket, I walked to the middle of the classroom and shook the bucket to randomize the responses. Then I explained, "I'm going to walk around your desks with my bucket. You will each choose a piece of paper. It will have something very serious written on it by someone who needs your advice on how to stay happy and optimistic. Their feelings have been hurt, and some have even cried because of what is written on that paper. Write a response complimenting them and encouraging them to do the right thing."

Once the responses were complete, several students volunteered to stand up and read their anonymous classmates' hurtful moments aloud followed by their solutions and encouragement.

Problems ranged from classic bullying incidents on the playground to students being told they were ugly or stupid to having their snacks taken from them. Responses varied from, "Kill them with kindness" to "Perhaps they're having a really bad day" to "You can ask them if they need any help" to "See if Mr. Duncan can talk to them."

The project created a room full of students aware of the serious problem in our classroom. It provided an opportunity for them to open up about what had hurt them, let others know their true feelings and intentions, and helped them understand their classmates' point of view. Most importantly, it allowed our classroom to better govern itself and my students to live by their own laws.

Fool Me Once, Shame on You; Fool Me Twice, Shame on Me

I was a daredevil as a kid. I climbed trees and did backflips off my friend's house onto mattresses. Talk about giving your parents a heart attack, but there weren't any parents around. One time I took a bowling ball and threw it off the roof and onto the sidewalk. To my surprise, the bowling ball wasn't damaged. On the other hand, the concrete sidewalk split from side to side. I still have scars on my back from slipping off that roof and rolling down into tree branches. My friends nonchalantly called me a monkey, and my cousin recalls me jumping from a tree branch nearly two stories high and successfully rolling the landing without getting hurt.

One day, I was walking out the back door of my friend's house on the way home to dinner with Grandpa, Grandma, and my brothers. Jake's older brother's friends were standing around in the backyard and suddenly turned towards me. One of them said, "Hey, you're the kid who can climb any tree, right?"

Not knowing what they were getting at, I confidently replied, "Yup, that's me."

"I'll give you $50.00 if you can climb up and touch the end of the branch." The teenager looked at his friends and smirked.

My mind raced. The tree was two times the height of the house. If I fell, injury was certain. Still, $50.00 was more money than I could imagine. At the age of seven, it might as well have been a million.

"Okay, I'm gonna do it. You just watch!"

I wrapped my arms around the trunk of the tree and simultaneously began moving my feet and arms. Pulling myself up to the smaller branches gave me access to the long overlying branch I needed to climb across and back. Slowly but surely I made it to the beginning of the tall, long branch. I could tell they were impressed when I glanced down. They were looking at one another and exchanging high fives.

"Okay, Josh," I told myself. "Just climb out over this branch. Do not think about how high up you are. You can do this! You're going to have $50.00 and your brothers will be so jealous!"

Motivated to get the bet over with and get home before Grandpa grounded me for coming in too late, I quickly scurried my way to the middle of the branch high above the green grass of the backyard.

About that time, without saying a word, the teenagers started walking away.

"Wait, where are you going?" I called.

They continued walking.

"Hey, come back! It won't take much longer for me to get down!" I yelled.

Then I realized what was going on. They had fooled me. I had let some older teenagers talk me into doing something they knew they couldn't do, and I'd actually believed they'd pay me for it. How could I be so dumb? Even if I saw them in the future, there was nothing to be done. They were bigger than me and everyone would laugh at how gullible I was.

I know what you're thinking—why didn't I tell my older brother?

Not a chance. He had enough trouble. It wouldn't be fair or smart to involve him. Besides, this was my responsibility to bear. As the old saying goes, "Fool me once, shame on you; fool me twice, shame on me."

Once I realized I'd been tricked, fear kicked in. One slip while turning my body around on the branch could cause me to fall and crack every bone in my body. I didn't want to scream for help because I was embarrassed. It was just me alone with my tears of disappointment, my shaky hands, and this tree I thought I was so cool to be able to climb.

I finally made it down safely and returned home for dinner with scratches all over my arms and legs and brown bark marks on my white shirt. "We were playing soccer and I fell pretty hard," I explained to Grandma and Grandpa.

I couldn't honestly count the number of times students dared other students to do something that ended up getting both parties in trouble. It was always the person who'd been fooled who suffered the biggest consequences. By the end of each year, my students knew what to expect if they made such a mistake twice.

"What do I always say?" I'd ask with a tilted head, eyes to the side and a smirk on my face.

"Fool me twice, shame on *meeeeeee*," each student would respond with a smile.

They were becoming self-aware and responsible for their own actions. It was okay to make mistakes. Yet once it happened over and over, you had to start reevaluating your approach. As Albert Einstein said, "Insanity is doing the same thing over and over and expecting a different result."

A common missing trait in underprivileged children is their ability to trust. This lack of trust is a result of seeing the people in their lives lie and then fail to take responsibility for their actions. This is how cold, senseless, and irresponsible humans develop, but it's sad, because every bad person was once a great child. Harsh environments make it impossible for children to see the light when negativity consumes them. These students become aggressors in part so that others won't be able to take advantage of them.

How many times have you heard a parent say, "If they hit you, hit them back?" While self-defense is certainly necessary at times, statements like this do not empower our youth with the knowledge they need to prevent fights in the first place. The power of being proactive just might be the greatest lesson our students can learn.

After living with my loving grandparents for several years, my brother and I were presented with the opportunity to live with my aunt. The best part about the move was that just a hundred yards behind her house was an elementary school with a huge field. It was open to the public and had a whopping six basketball hoops! I was in heaven. The court hosted up to 30 people at a time, and I was going to make sure I was there for every second of it. Besides that, my aunt would take my brother and me out to eat several times a week. My grandparents could only afford to do this once every two weeks!

As crazy as it might seem, I didn't enjoy this new privilege as much as I thought I would. I would eat up my food as fast as possible and anxiously wait for everyone else to finish, hoping I could make it to the courts before sunset.

During the hot Texas summers, the court schedule changed. Most of the regulars were on vacation or simply wanted to avoid the heat. Two teens about five years older than me came to the court one evening and asked if they could play a game with me. I responded "Sure" and suggested we play the popular game of 21 where the first player to 21 points wins. Just as in Black Jack, if you go over 21, you bust and have to start over or are set back with lower points. I won all three games of 21 despite being smaller than they were and five years younger. We shared laughs and they even thanked me for letting them play.

The very next evening, I was shooting baskets by myself. In my mind, thousands of fans were watching as I dribbled out the clock and took the last second shot, leading my team to victory. These shots never grew old, but I definitely preferred to practice my heroics on real people. I enjoyed being younger than my competition and beating them. We tend to enjoy what we're good at, and my forte was sports.

From the corner of my eye and the opposite direction of my house, I saw two teenagers walking through the fence from the street heading for the basketball court. Although they were two football fields away, I immediately recognized them. It was the same guys from the day before.

"What's up?" I heard one of them call as they both raised their arms in the sky. Letting them know I remembered them from the day before, I raised my hands too and replied with a "What's up?" of my own. In anticipation of getting to play with some cool kids again and maybe gain new friendships, I started to dribble between my legs and behind my back as I faded away from the basket and jumped as high as I could, shooting swish after swish.

"What's up, homie. You got a problem?" One of the teenag-ers said as soon as they reached the basketball courts.

I could sense something was wrong. Their eyes were red and their tone was different. They both surrounded me, leaving only inches between my body and theirs. Next thing I knew, I was getting pushed back and forth until tears began to fill my eyes. How could two people who had been so friendly the day before now want to hurt me? I knew I could defend myself from one of them, but two would be impossible. They were older and bigger.

"What's wrong? What did I do? I'm sorry," I quickly said before they started swinging.

My temperament wasn't aggressive. Unlike my brothers, I was sensitive. I didn't want to fight. I didn't want people who knew where I'd be every day to hold a grudge against me. I had learned through my brother that it's never-ending, that one fight only leads to more.

The teenager responded, "You raised your hands to us. You raised your head up. You never do that to us! That means you want to fight, and we will **** you up."

"I'm sorry! I didn't know! I remembered you from yester-day and thought you were saying hi by raising your hands. I was saying hi back. I really didn't know."

The truth was, I did know. I knew that they were illogical. I knew that raising my hands to them and moving my head up didn't mean I wanted to fight. My friends and I did it all the time. It was a popular gesture at that time, especially in urban culture. I also already knew there was nothing to gain by argu-ing with them. By playing by their rules, I could get out of the situation. Mark Twain said it best: "If you argue with a fool, it makes two of them." In this case, it would have made three.

The two teenagers looked at one another, talked a moment, and turned to me. "Never let us catch you doing that again, homie."

As they walked away, I let out a sigh of relief. I had almost been jumped by two bullies looking to cause trouble and had somehow found a way to escape.

After that, these two boys would sometimes come to the park and ask if they could play with me. I would hesitantly say yes and make sure my demeanor wasn't too aggressive. My experience with these two teens forever changed my nonverbal communication. I never raise my hands in the air. I never nod my head up and backwards when acknowledging anyone. If you think about it, it is disrespectful. Instead, I nod my head down quickly before lifting it up while maintaining eye contact and giving a warm smile.

Parents, teachers, and schools are becoming more proactive about trying to prevent bullying, but students still face thousands of bullying incidents each year. Ignoring bullying doesn't make it go away. Instead, kids need guidance—parental guidance, whether from parents or teachers—so that they know how to avoid and/or respond to these situations. They can team up with a buddy. They can stay near their homes or schools. If possible, an adult can talk to the bully and work to build trust. In all likelihood, the bully doesn't know what trust is.

Changing the life of a young bully can in turn help turn hundreds of other lives around. I've always believed that anger is a fake emotion, a cover-up for disappointment and sadness.

Bullies are usually the living epitome of this, but if we don't guide our kids to know how to handle bullies, they can fall prey to this behavior, too. A little guidance, whether from teachers, parents, or both, can go a long way towards keeping kids safe and preventing bullying in the first place.

CHAPTER 19:

TELL 'EM WHY

Every person's map of the world is as unique as their thumbprint.
There are no two people alike. No two people who understand the
same sentence the same way...So in dealing with people, you try
not to fit them to your concept of what they should be.

Milton H. Erickson

When I was a kid, I used to raise my hand after every single question my teacher asked. When she didn't call on me, I became confused. I had proven that I knew the answers, so why did she keep calling other students? Their answers were wrong half the time!

My patience quickly turned to frustration. I quit raising my hand as much, and soon I decided to only raise my hand if no one else was raising theirs. This was how I would prove my intelligence and impress the teacher. Meanwhile, I wondered why my teacher encouraged me to participate if she wasn't going to call on me to answer the questions.

Decades later, with my role reversed, I saw lots of little Joshua's anxious to share what they knew. These same students raised their hands every time I asked a question, and they had the correct answer 99% of the time. But guess what? I rarely called on them!

What an ironic turnaround. As teacher, I repeated the same "mistake" my teacher had made. Or was what my teacher had done okay after all?

Teachers love to give grades. Looking back, most of my teachers did an okay job of calling on students with their hands raised. If I had to grade them, I'd give them a passing grade of 70%. Here's why.

Dealing appropriately with students requires communication. As happened with me, I began to see my enthusiastic students volunteering less and reacting with frustration because they weren't called upon in large group discussions. Recognizing their growing negativity, I immediately pulled these students aside and explained my reasoning.

"I'm working to develop a classroom of problem solvers," I said. "Do you think the majority of the classroom knows the answer or does not know the answer?"

"Most of them do not know the right answer," Henry responded. "Sometimes only two people raise their hands!"

I replied, "And if I call on you every time, is this going to encourage them to volunteer or will it make them think, 'Well, Henry will just answer it for us?'"

Another student chimed in, "They will just let Henry answer it."

The key is communication. I complimented my students for their willingness to participate, and I entitled them to be classroom leaders. My talented students went from frustrated to proud!

I told them, "Let's give our friends the opportunity to brainstorm. Let's give them the opportunity to build upon their thoughts and most importantly to give wrong answers because misconceptions are our greatest teaching tools. When I ask a highly advanced question, I want to encourage you to step up to the plate and volunteer to answer it. Know that when I do not call on you it isn't because I don't appreciate your answers. It's because I'm looking to advance the entire class and there are just a few of you who can answer almost any question I ask. Thanks for understanding. You are awesome." The lesson was complete.

Our open lines of communication allowed my leaders to keep their confidence, helped them understand that they weren't doing anything wrong by volunteering every time, and helped them understand why I didn't call on them.

Likewise, as I've mentioned, I often reminded my students that the greatest teachers teach students how to teach themselves. I often encouraged my students to do research projects, and I encouraged my advanced students to go ahead in the book and learn lessons on their own.

I shared, "When you are an adult and want to start a business, is someone going to come to you with a silver platter, take the lid off revealing the task at hand, and give you an instruction manual on how to start the business correctly?"

Of course, "No" is the response.

I continued, "Then we can agree that you have to figure it out yourself. Any questions you have, I encourage you to do the research and bring your idea to life. The internet is powerful. When you want to accomplish something, you have to research the proper steps. Can you learn how to do it yourself through books and the internet? Do you know someone else who has already accomplished your goal? Can you sign up for classes?"

I would have given my former teachers A's if they had explained why I wasn't called on and helped me understand their responsibility to teach all their students, not just one. Kids should understand that without being told, you say? Maybe in a perfect world, but it's not a perfect world. Tell 'em why.

CHAPTER 20:

WHAT MENTORS CAN DO

A good teacher can inspire hope, ignite the imagination,
and instill a love of learning.

Brad Henry

My mom was never in a position to be my mentor. My dad was never in a position to be my mentor. A couple of my brothers were never in a position to be my mentor. Yet I learned more from these four individuals than anyone else. My aunt always says it best: "Don't just focus on what is good but also focus on what is bad and decide what you would do differently."

I knew what *not* to do by living through the hardships and heartbreak my immediate family caused, but this didn't necessarily mean I knew what the next step was. From a young age, I studied adults. I studied their interactions with one another, especially couples and their children. I always wondered, how do great relationships develop? Once they develop, how do they function? How do children who have great parents mature?

What difference does having great parents make in their development and outcomes?

My grandparents were my first mentors. Grandpa taught me that a man can be kind. He always created laughter in a room full of strangers. He was strict at times yet he also knew when someone needed a hug or words of encouragement. He loved his wife and stayed loyal to her as they raised four children plus multiple grandchildren. Grandma spoiled my brothers and me even in her old age. She worked a full-time job, cooked, cleaned, made pies for her friends, and was the breadwinner in our small home. My grandparents represented love.

My aunt was my second mentor. Grandma spoiled us and didn't make us do housework. I hated chores, and when I moved in with my aunt, I asked what I would get in return for doing them. "You get a roof over your head and food on the table," she answered firmly.

My aunt did much more than put a roof over my head. She sent me to sports camps, gave us theme park season passes, and bought us new clothes for every season of the year. My aunt also taught me manners. She taught me small things, including how spitting on the cement or passing gas and burping in front of others was unacceptable and not how a respectful man or woman behaved. My aunt would be the first to tell you, these were tough habits to break.

I also learned to dress appropriately for special occasions and to say "Yes, sir" and "Yes, ma'am." I learned that throwing a fit didn't mean I was right or that I was going to get my way; this in turn taught me that the world didn't stop if my world stopped. This could be the single most valuable lesson I ever learned. My aunt represented discipline.

My family friends were my third mentors. As a junior in high school, I packed up my bags and moved to a new city to pursue a higher education and expand my athletic ability at a private school. Leaving my aunt's driveway was the first time I ever drove by myself. This incredible symbolism marked the beginning of a new journey for me. I had become accustomed to being one of the brightest in the classroom, but in my new school, I was in the middle of the crowd. In my advanced classes, I was at the bottom.

A mother whose son attended my school offered me a bedroom in their home and took me in as if I were her own. Looking back, this was a large risk. I enjoyed basketball culture, listened to loud music, and wore baggy clothing that often carried a negative connotation. My immediate family's criminal record was as lengthy as a corporate company's terms and conditions. What if I was a bad role model to her son? I am forever grateful she took the risk.

I had basketball training before school and practice after. As soon as I made it home, I would work on my homework until 10:00 or 11:00 and then wake up the next day to do it again. One evening, I walked downstairs with tears in my eyes, on the verge of giving up. My new housemom encouraged me to keep going, saying it would only get easier with time and that the work I was doing would make the challenge of college less overwhelming. I wiped the tears from my eyes and finished up my work. She was right. Everything began to get easier, and I found strength in my ability to overcome obstacles.

My friendship with her son quickly became more of a brotherhood. My friendships with my fellow classmates also grew as did my maturity and understanding of how big the world was.

I worked during the summer and was allowed to make my own decisions, making mistakes and growing from them. In this time, I grew exponentially.

My first real girlfriend was intelligent, artsy, and loving. She exposed me to new music and helped me adjust to the new culture around me. She liked many of the same things I did and met me in the middle on other things. She allowed me the opportunity to open up to change. I began to dress differently and carry myself with class. Her parents were my first role models, displaying what a great relationship looked like. They were kind to one another, did each other favors, and calmly spoke about their disagreements. In short, they taught me how a man and a woman should treat one another.

A coach and close mentor carved the path that allowed me to develop the confidence to be a teacher. He was a former college athlete, maintained a high level of physical activity, smiled often, and worked as a second grade elementary teacher. I saw his joy and wanted to share what he was experiencing. Even today, nearly a decade later, Jimmy Agnew continues to positively influence others. He founded the non-profit organization One Wheel Many Children in Austin, Texas. One of my favorite lines from the organization's vision statement is, "We understand that it is not about preparing the path for the child but about preparing the child for the path."

My family friends represented independence.

I was lucky. In my experience, most students lack sufficient mentors and role models. Without mentors, most students lack the knowledge to understand that they can be different from the people they grow up with. Encouraging students to find mentors and then to study and learn from the people they look up to helps equip students with the tools they need to turn their dreams into reality. It is much easier to find the courage to do something when you know someone else who has already done it. I can singlehandedly attribute the majority of my business success to my continuous search for mentors who are happy to share their knowledge with me.

If I could give only three words of advice to my students, those words would be, "Find a mentor."

As for my fellow teachers: *be* a mentor.

CHAPTER 21:

HOW HAVE I DONE?

A TEACHER'S LETTER TO HIS CLASSROOM

Don't ever mistake my silence for ignorance, my calmness for acceptance, or my kindness for weakness.

Carson Konhoff

Every teacher has a class that conjures up visions of early retirement. The perfect (or not-so-perfect) combination of students creates and in turn requires an energy level that's impossible to maintain. Halfway through a year that nearly did me in, I asked my class to join me on the front carpet. Although I taught math and science, it was time for me to read them something. I rewarded them with extra credit for taking notes as I read the following letter.

Good evening, friends,

As your teacher, I know all 23 of you are attentive to me. I might not always have your full attention, but I know you're watching. My voice is the one you soak in like a sponge, taking the knowledge it contains and the guidance it directs. The thousand-plus hours you spend watching me in the span of a school year is certain to leave an imprint on you like fossils in sediment.

So how have I done?

It's the Friday before holiday break. Our spirits are high, each particle of our bodies are as wild as a gaseous state of matter. A normal routine—lining up appropriately—is forgotten or ignored. Requests to rotate from one educational activity to another are disregarded. A shout disperses from a single vertex of the room and catches on like protons on a warm load of laundry just out of the dryer.

Another day, we are rewarded with recess for an incredible 15 minutes, something I rarely experienced in my elementary years. I signal that it's time to return to class. A minute passes, and a football is thrown across the court. A basketball takes a reckless weave towards the basket, almost hitting our friends in line. The one basketball that actually makes it in line is quickly swiped away, causing it to slowly bounce back to the court.

We are back in class. I assign word problems that align to real-world scenarios. Most of you don't even pick up a pencil. Unless taught one-on-one and consistently reminded of the importance of problem solving, I seldom witness an attempt to solve the task I have presented. Instead, you engage in side conversations and ignore your responsibilities.

I hear you call each other names such as "fat," "ugly," "stupid," and sometimes even worse. Students scream at one another, push, and cry tears of hurt feelings.

So, how have I done as your teacher? Let's think back to recess and the need to line up. Watching you, I searched for eyes that would make contact with mine. Five of you did. I smiled and complimented your poise. I truly appreciated you listening to my directions.

At that point, I gained the attention of five more of you who inched into the tightly formed line.

You must first be able to follow before you can lead, I told you. I am impressed by my leaders, I said. When you are older, you deserve to be in positions of leadership and to have great jobs because you can handle it.

Eight more students adjusted their posture and gave me the signal that they were ready to travel through a school of hundreds happily, respectfully, and maturely. Five students still hadn't joined the group.

Had I shouted yet? Had I frightened my dependable friends standing gingerly in line? Had my voice risen to a level of dominance? Had I roared at the disrespectful behaviors and shown you that the louder person wins the conversation?

I had not. If I'd screamed, you would have heard my voice and stopped out of fear. I would have taught you that the stronger and louder a person is, the better chance they have of winning. I would have taught you that anger conquers respect, and that just isn't true.

Speaking directly to my five friends talking out of line, I told them their voices were distracting others. I asked them to join us in line. I told them that when they walked calmly, spoke respectfully, and recognized social norms, they would be successful. I reminded everyone to smile. I smiled, letting you all know that great behavior, not negative behavior, determines how I feel.

The next day, we again had trouble getting to our destination because we ignored the signal to line up when recess was over. I thanked my friends in the front of the line for lining up. I sent a firm reminder that I would appreciate a civil line and was again ignored by nearly 10 students. I confronted an argument between two students when I saw a boy pushed up against the wall. I heard, "He knocked the ball out of my hands first," "He was playing rough," and "He called me a name." The blame game took off faster than a Space X shuttle.

What did I do? I listened. I heard hurt and sadness. I reminded these students that anger is the emotion we feel to cover up sadness. I explained that the only reason we hurt other people is that we are hurt ourselves. The two friends joined the line and we entered the building.

What happens when you don't do your work? Do I scream at you and tell you how unintelligent you are and how you will never become anything great because you will not work?

I do not. I tell you how great you are. I tell you that the world is full of choices and that those choices are yours. I tell you that if anyone ever tells you that there isn't a choice, you shouldn't believe them. I teach you to take pride in your work because each and every one of you is unique and there will never be another one of you as long as mankind roams this earth. Day by day, I build confidence. Brick by brick, I build a strong foundation. Hooray!

Wait! How many students are solving real-world math problems about money? Just five? No, I see 10 students working diligently! Wait, we haven't just doubled five; we've now doubled 10! We now have a classroom in which 21 out of 23 students are giving each and every problem their best effort.

So tell me, how have I done? Has my optimism worked better for you than negativity and screaming? How has it worked when people call you names? As your teacher, I've witnessed more tears than a ninja in a room full of onions. I have seen children hold their heads down from the beginning of the school day until the last bell rings because of mean words someone said to them.

Have I run over to the suspect and screamed at them for their hurtful and reckless words? Have I told them they're terrible and sent them out of the classroom to stand with their noses on the wall?

I have not. As tears streamed down your face, I focused on you. I asked you to be strong and reminded you, "You are amazing." I asked you to think about the kind people in your life instead of giving the negative people power over you. I told you that your true friends need your smile and that the people who are hurtful can never take that away.

Only then did I speak to the suspect, explain that you were hurt, and ask for an explanation of these hurtful words.

It's always the same old reasons. Either their feelings were hurt by someone else or they were afraid of what they didn't know and didn't take the time to learn more. I didn't scream.

I explained that we're all different. I showed you my beautiful smile with crooked teeth. I shared with you my "silver fox" and "silver back" representing my prematurely graying hair. I laughed as I let you hear the strange accent in my voice. I told you not to be afraid of what you don't understand. I told you not to fear the different and the unknown. I asked you to embrace it and to see the unique beauty in the imperfections that make us so different from everyone else.

Remember that scuffle we had during a soccer game when students were pushing, kicking, and screaming? How did I handle that as I ran over to the racial name calling?

I explained that we needed to understand something: two people had a problem with one another during a soccer game. That was it. It had nothing to do with race. Even so, someone decided to immaturely call a person of a different ethnicity a racial slur, and that is unacceptable. Intelligent people fix their problems by debating. When we start name calling because we can't use words fluently, that is a sign of a lack of intelligence. I asked you to learn from this mistake, and you did. This never happened again.

I once spoke to you as a class and asked you a simple question. I asked, are you going to respect the person who screams at you and fills you with fear, or are you going to respect the person who speaks to you kindly and builds your confidence? Each and every one of you said you would respect the person who treats you with kindness.

I challenge you to do just that today. I challenge you to become those kind and respectful men and women of the future. Life is chaotic. Without dilemmas in our classroom, we wouldn't have any lessons to learn. Thank you for reminding me of that.

As soon as I finished reading, my students started clapping. I received multiple group hugs and was even told, "Wow, you're a really good writer. Why do you teach math and science again?"

I think I was able to get the point across. It was a difficult year, but I wasn't going to let them know it. And yes, it was worth it.

CONCLUSION:

PROBLEMS AND SOLUTIONS

Do not bring up a problem without presenting a solution.

Teachers aren't treated as well as they should be, yet they're the most dedicated professionals on the planet.

The public school system could be structured better, but some of our nation's greatest minds are working furiously to solve the problem at hand.

Difficult home circumstances highly impact youth, yet schools are administering mentor programs that pair students with successful adults, increasing their chances of success.

Poverty in lower income areas is a vicious cycle that spreads faster than it can be solved, but organizations are fighting tooth and nail to provide opportunities to as many students as they can.

How do we solve the problems so pervasive in lower income school districts?

Appreciate the Good

The first step is to make sure we don't ignore the great things happening around us.

Police officers still pull over to help change a tire, strangers still find lost wallets and use the ID inside to find the rightful owners, and people still tip hard-working waiters and waitresses.

Volunteers still put smiles on the faces of the elderly, paramedics and doctors still work overtime to save lives, and foundations continue granting wishes to the terminally ill.

I could write another book simply focusing on all the good around us, and perhaps I will, because most people have been conditioned to ignore the positive and focus on the negative.

Daily acts of kindness by the millions of great people around the world should not be overlooked or forgotten just because of the bad actions of a statistically much smaller population. It is the great people who deserve our energy, not the bad. Great people go out of their way to give hugs and words of encouragement. Great people go out of their way to start non-profit organizations that benefit their communities. Great people lose sleep, relationships, and sometimes jeopardize their own happiness to make sure those around them are taken care of.

We often talk about the people who hurt us. We often talk about the things that scare us. We often talk about those with evil intentions.

I'm not suggesting we ignore the bad in the world. I'm saying the best way to combat it is to give life to the good!

Poverty is real, and it's scary.

Racism is real, and it's scary.

Crime is real, and it's scary.

War is real, and it's scary.

Death is real, and it's scary.

But these things don't mean great people don't exist. They're everywhere. My aunt once told me, "You're going to find exactly what you're looking for." If we look only for the bad, this is exactly what we'll find. If we take the time to focus on the good happening around us, we'll be amazed at how quickly life will transform.

So be careful next time you watch the news. Whether you're a child or an adult, a student or a teacher, be selective about what you choose to listen to because it will impact who you are and the person you are becoming.

Become a Mentor; Map a Path to Success

The second step to helping lower income students thrive is a familiar one—supporting mentorship programs or volunteering to be a mentor yourself. Remember Lauren who learned to create bracelets, purses, and much more by watching creative people on the internet? Remember John and his influence with the young ladies because of the mentors he became acquainted with in the books he read? Remember Joe and his mentors, the rappers singing on the radio, who had such a large influence on him? Remember society's perception of success and the athletes, musicians, and movie stars we often look up to? Those around us have a great influence on who we become because they help us see possibilities we might otherwise remain ignorant of.

Many of our students follow the path their parents took. If Dad was a truck driver, his son becomes a truck driver. If Mom was a teacher, her daughter becomes a teacher. There's nothing wrong with this unless the situation is one in which Dad went to prison or Mom is addicted to drugs, which all too often is the case in lower income school districts.

Breaking this vicious cycle has nothing to do with how much free food, free clothes, free ipads, free iPhones, and free school supplies are given away. It has nothing to do with a visitor pulling up in a fancy car on career day wearing a $10,000 watch.

Mentorship boils down to having qualified mentors who are willing to spend valuable hours with our youth. During this time, the mentor gets to know the student and begins to make a checklist of the child's strengths. Once admiration, trust, and friendship are built, the mentor can begin talking about options based upon the strengths they've observed.

Say Lucia is a great artist. The issue is, she's drawing in class rather than completing her work. The common response is to take the paper and throw it away since the student isn't on task. With this approach, the risk of Lucia becoming a janitor like her mother drastically increases.

Instead, the mentor can use a much more effective approach, one with positive power. If the teacher is also a mentor, he or she might say, "Lucia, this is such a beautiful drawing! I'm going to place it on my desk, and after we finish this assignment, I want to hear all about it!"

This response doesn't reject the child's passion, which would cause her to become defensive and unwilling to complete the task at hand. Instead, the compliment encourages her, and she's now more likely to finish her work and even listen to reason when asked to save her art work for classroom breaks and before or after school.

Mentorship doesn't stop here. Whether it's Lucia's teacher, an older student, or a qualified successful adult, the mentor must help Lucia understand how to pursue a career in art. The first step is passing and graduating from elementary school, middle school, and high school. The second step is knowing the careers great artists typically pursue as adults. Many become art teachers. Some convert their art to digital form and become graphic designers. Others become architects and engineers. Still others continue to make unique art and attempt to sell it. These artists succeed by studying business and marketing, which gives them the ability to sell their work.

Every qualified mentor brings knowledge and ideas the previous mentor didn't have. The more mentors children have, the better their chances of succeeding, thanks to their newfound knowledge of "how to succeed."

It really is simple when you think about it. Poverty, high crime rates in lower income neighborhoods, children following in their parents' footsteps—all these things are a cycle. If a child is never exposed to the world outside their own disadvantaged bubble, they are likely to stay in that bubble. It is very difficult for the cycle to be broken from the inside; it has to be broken from the outside.

As an educator, teach what you're required to teach, but be knowledgeable of career opportunities and your students' strengths and interests. It just might save their lives.

Be the Change You Wish to See in the World

The third step to finding a solution to problems inherent in lower income school districts is refusing to wait for others to make things better. In other words, if there isn't a way, then create one.

Albert Einstein said, "The world is a dangerous place to live; not because of the people who are evil, but because of the people who don't do anything about it."

Each time you read a new post on Facebook that makes you feel sad, angry, or emotionally compromised, counter it by doing something productive rather than engaging in a social media battle that will do nothing to change the issue at hand.

Let's say you're unhappy with an elected politician. Is posting something negative going to make a difference given that the outcome has already been decided? The answer is no. Instead, research your favorite up-and-coming political figures and potential candidates and begin promoting them by pointing out their policies and what will make them well qualified to serve. This approach is more productive than wasting time trying to convince people on social media that they're wrong when in reality it's way too late to change their minds.

If bullying is an issue in your classroom, don't just stand around and complain to your coworkers and staff saying you need more help. Notice I said "do not just," because asking for help is the first thing you should do. You can also make change by researching helpful class activities, rearranging the classroom, and sharing stories about how you were once bullied or even bullied someone else and how it made you feel.

Recall how, when I was having bullying issues in the classroom, I created the bucket bullying activity?

If you feel that teachers aren't supported as much as they should be, that standardized tests are unfair, or that the curriculum isn't what should be taught, do not seek change by gossiping with your fellow staff members about how unjust the system is. Write your own articles. Send a letter to the state and the federal government. Create unique lessons that intertwine what you think is most important to teach with what you're required to teach. Get your master's degree in administration and pursue a position in education. Get your degree in law and fight for what you think is the best answer to our complex school system of millions of teachers and students. I challenge you to do more than just talk about it and complain on social media.

There will always be something to complain about, but if you think about it, without a game plan for action, complaining is a waste of time. If you aren't sure what you can do, ask a friend or co-worker and come up with some ideas. If you continuously hear others around you complaining, pleasantly challenge them by asking, "Can you suggest a solution?"

I encourage you to keep an open mind when it comes to your students, your staff, your curriculum, your pay structure, and so much more. All change is uncomfortable, even when it's for the better. That's why it comes with growing pains.

In order to make the changes we need, it's best to evaluate everyone's opinion. Unfortunately, it's becoming the norm to only give support in the form of all or nothing. This approach might be loyal, but it isn't always logical. Perhaps a staff member has a great curriculum idea but lacks an effective behavior system. Do not completely dismiss other people's ideas because you disagree with an aspect of something they say or do. Integrate their great ideas into your classroom and leave what you disagree with alone. You probably don't agree with everything I've mentioned in this book, but I hope you'll be able to take some of the lessons you think are valuable and use them to benefit others.

Making change in the world doesn't rely on being stubborn. It doesn't even rely on always being correct. It relies on researching, listening, learning, and taking action. Making the greatest change often means having the patience to listen to someone you don't agree with. Although they might be wrong, you can still learn from them. Why do they feel that way, what about their environment has influenced their thinking, and, most importantly, what can you do to productively share your own beliefs instead of focusing on what you don't agree with?

Regardless of where you live and work, whether you impact one child at a time or an entire classroom, I hope you'll join me in working to improve the lives and opportunities of lower income students. Teachers can change the trajectory of these kids. Be that teacher. They need your help, they deserve it, and everything about our world will be better for it.

ABOUT THE AUTHOR

Josh Duncan is a former elementary school teacher who was inspired to enter the classroom because he wanted to help kids who reminded him of himself—an impoverished child whose parents and brothers were incarcerated, who didn't know where his next meal was coming from, and whose toes poked through the holes of his shoes. After teaching for four and a half years, Josh made the leap from classroom to CEO in order to forge connections with the business community and create a network of influential leaders. His goal is to make real change in lower income classrooms. He hopes to influence thousands of teachers who in turn will reach many more children than he could in a single classroom. His debut book *Lessons from the Back of the Line: How Teachers Change the Trajectory of Lower Income Students* creates awareness and offers insight into the challenges lower income students face. The CEO and founder of the marketing firm Software Blueprint, LLC and the founder of the non-profit organization Ascension Leadership Group, Josh lives in Dallas, Texas.

www.ingramcontent.com/pod-product-compliance
Lightning Source LLC
Chambersburg PA
CBHW052037090426
42739CB00010B/1946